The Language of Spirit

Aboriginal Medium Shawn Leonard

Copyright © 2018 Aboriginal Medium Shawn Leonard.

All rights reserved. No part of this book may be used or reproduced by any means, graphic, electronic, or mechanical, including photocopying, recording, taping or by any information storage retrieval system without the written permission of the author except in the case of brief quotations embodied in critical articles and reviews.

Scriptures Taken from the King James Version of the Bible.

Balboa Press books may be ordered through booksellers or by contacting:

Balboa Press
A Division of Hay House
1663 Liberty Drive
Bloomington, IN 47403
www.balboapress.com
1 (877) 407-4847

Because of the dynamic nature of the Internet, any web addresses or links contained in this book may have changed since publication and may no longer be valid. The views expressed in this work are solely those of the author and do not necessarily reflect the views of the publisher, and the publisher hereby disclaims any responsibility for them.

The author of this book does not dispense medical advice or prescribe the use of any technique as a form of treatment for physical, emotional, or medical problems without the advice of a physician, either directly or indirectly. The intent of the author is only to offer information of a general nature to help you in your quest for emotional and spiritual well-being. In the event you use any of the information in this book for yourself, which is your constitutional right, the author and the publisher assume no responsibility for your actions.

Any people depicted in stock imagery provided by Getty Images are models, and such images are being used for illustrative purposes only. Certain stock imagery © Getty Images.

Print information available on the last page.

ISBN: 978-1-5043-9963-0 (sc)
ISBN: 978-1-5043-9965-4 (hc)
ISBN: 978-1-5043-9964-7 (e)

Library of Congress Control Number: 2018902795

Balboa Press rev. date: 05/14/2018

"Shawn Leonard has a true gift, a unique ability to see beyond what most of us are capable of seeing, and his willingness to share that with the world is a blessing to us all. I highly recommend his work as he has personally delivered to me personal and profound insight." - Serena Dyer

"As Shawn shared messages from loved ones with my mother, I witnessed her receiving a priceless gift; the gift of unshakable hope and reassurance that life exceeds well beyond what we can see and touch. In that moment she gained an acceptance of something much greater than fear or doubt. I'm not sure even he realizes how profound his gifts are; I'm forever grateful." - Dawn Sinclair

"Spent twenty years in denial and agony dealing with my mother's tragic passing, until that unexpected encounter with Shawn. The day that changed my life and the way I approach life and any encounters that come my way" - Daniel Glover

"An inspiration, a heart of gold, a breath of fresh air and someone who is able to bring so much closure to broken hearts." - Laura Coelho

"I cried tears of joy the entire reading knowing it was my son delivering messages through him. The most healing experience I have had since his passing." - Cindy Lewis

Contents

Foreword....................... xi
Introduction.................... xv

Chapter 1 I Needed to Forget................. 1
Chapter 2 The Dark and the Light............. 8
Chapter 3 Farewell to Nova Scotia............14
Chapter 4 Hello Alberta.....................20
Chapter 5 Spirit Talks......................25
Chapter 6 Blue Jays and Dimes...............33
Chapter 7 Searching for My Spirit...........41
Chapter 8 Travelling Back in Time...........47
Chapter 9 Ghosts at The Rouge...............55
Chapter 10 Faith Leads Me Home...............59
Chapter 11 Paper Messages by Day, Spirit by Night.....64
Chapter 12 Thy Will Be Done..................68
Chapter 13 Spirit Communication..............74
Chapter 14 Leaving and Finding...............79

Chapter 15	Paranormal and Pirates	83
Chapter 16	Connecting at Costco	89
Chapter 17	A Physical Encounter with My Guides	93
Chapter 18	My First Eagle Feather	97
Chapter 19	The Big Nudge	100
Chapter 20	An Elder Appears	102
Chapter 21	The Importance of Validation	106
Chapter 22	Courageous Parents	111
Chapter 23	An Unexpected Voice	117
Chapter 24	Dreams and Gabriel	121
Chapter 25	Guidance from the Masters	125
Chapter 26	Wendy Kelly Dawn Hare	131
Chapter 27	Only a Thought Away	136
Chapter 28	A Visit from an Old Friend	139
Chapter 29	Signs from Spirit	142
Chapter 30	The Language of Spirit	146
Chapter 31	Intention	154
Chapter 32	Native Culture and Spirituality	158
Chapter 33	Your Journey	165

This book is dedicated to every person I have connected to throughout my journey, as every single one has helped me become the person I am. To my father James, for the ultimate sacrifice of leaving this world to show me the light; and to my spirit guides, Sam and Victoria.

I especially dedicate this book to every spirit who entrusted me with their messages.

Wela'lioq Kesaluloq (Mi'kmaq)

Thanks and love to all

Foreword

I met Shawn in 2010, when my daughter was two. She still wasn't sleeping through the night, and I was sleep deprived. I had begun writing my book, *Be Feel Think Do: A Memoir* (published by Hay House in 2017), and I felt as though I wasn't getting anywhere. The more tired I became, the more impatient I became with myself.

On one particularly stressful morning my husband saw the discouragement on my face and said, "Why don't you take a couple of days away, get some sleep, catch up on some writing, and take care of yourself."

Wow ... what an idea! (Funny how we young mothers don't see taking time off as an option). So, I booked a couple of nights in a hotel, had some most delightful sleep, and got a lot of writing done. As for self-care, I reached out to a friend who knew many healers in the city and she recommended I connect with this new medium in town: Shawn Leonard. I trusted this friend, so I reached out and booked a session. He came to the hotel the very next day.

When Shawn walked in he felt very familiar. I had just met him, yet somehow I already trusted him. We sat down and he began to share information (which he couldn't have possibly known) about my grandmother, who passed away when I was fifteen. I was blown away, and so happy to connect with her in this way. Granny and I were close. I felt her presence from the other side of the veil the day she died, and since then she has been my guide. She knew coming through Shawn that day would be significant, and I was grateful to Shawn for bringing her forward.

We talked about my writing. Shawn told me I also had a guide named Vishnu, who was helping me with my book. I hadn't heard that name before, but I was open to the possibility of meeting a new spiritual ally. Then Shawn said, "Wait, hold on. You don't know him as Vishnu. You know him as Timmy." My jaw dropped; I was stunned. I had completely forgotten about the Care Bear I had as a little girl, with whom I had an ongoing conversation. He was more than just a stuffed animal to me; he was real. A friend and a confidant. On his ear he had a little red plastic heart with the letters TM. Growing up in rural Québec I didn't know that TM meant "Trademark". I assumed it was related to his name, so I called him Timmy.

I had never told anyone about Timmy, and he wasn't on my mind. So how could Shawn have known his name? It was incredible, and it meant a great deal to me. Writing is a lonely process, but I now felt the presence and support of my old companion.

Shawn's gift of clairaudience is unlike anything I have before seen—and I have worked with my share of mediums! He knows, without a shadow of a doubt, the names of the spirits with whom he communicates. He does not guess, and he does not fish for answers.

Shawn's messages from departed loved ones are incredibly healing. His insights act as a balm, soothing the heart of a grieving family member or a friend. In an instant a parent lets go of guilt, a child knows they are still loved, and a spouse is comforted; all rest assured there is more love and joy ahead. That is the power of Shawn's work: he helps those of us who have lost someone let go of our fear, anger, and despair. He opens up new possibilities within ourselves.

When my dear friend, Wayne Dyer, passed away on August 30, 2015, my grief was profound. Shawn was one of the first to share direct messages from Wayne, and those communications greatly helped to heal my sadness. They lifted me up and helped deepen my connection to spirit, reinforcing my commitment to my path.

During his time on this earth Wayne would get very excited about synchronicities and mysterious signs from the spirit world. He gravitated toward the mystical, and toward anyone who could give an undeniable glimpse into the world beyond the veil. I know, had he met Shawn, he would have adored him; not just for his incredible talent as a spirit talker, but also for the kind, good-hearted, authentic, and down-to-earth man Shawn is.

You, too, can develop your ability to communicate with spirit. If you wish to learn how to refine your innate gift as a spirit talker, this book is for you. Through the authentic sharing of his journey, Shawn will guide you in learning to trust yourself and understanding the language of spirit. I trust you will be inspired by this wonderful book, as I have been inspired by my dear friend. Life feels fuller, and pain easier to bear, when his spiritual wisdom finds a place in your heart.

In Divine Love, always,
Anne Bérubé, PhD

Introduction

Kwe', welta'si na' pekisin (meaning, "Hello, I'm glad you came" in Mi'kmaq).

My name is Shawn Leonard, and I am an Aboriginal medium. I, like yourself, have been on an incredible journey. Life is about discovering one's self and one's purpose in life, answering the question as to why we are here. As early as I can remember, I have been on a journey to discover where we go after our physical life ends.

I never thought, in a million years, I would be sharing my story up to this point in my life. I didn't set out as a young man to be the person I am today. My goals were to have a well-paying job, to create a family I could love and support, and to live my life as I was raised by my parents. This is how I envisioned what a happy life was supposed to look.

I now know, through this incredible gift of life, that we all have a purpose and a calling deep within our souls: to be the best we can, and to learn unconditional love for ourselves and for others. It is through this love my calling and life's purpose became known. Through the love of those people I had lost in this physical life, and who visited both from and within the light which surrounds us all.

The wisdom and insight I have gained from my experiences have been nothing short of life-changing. In fact, they have been so incredibly life-altering that the trajectory of my time on this physical earth has become so clear as to change every aspect of how I see reality. It made me realize how we are all connected—even after supposed death—to the point I no longer believe in it. Death is an illusion!

We all have been taught, in the scientific method, that energy cannot be destroyed, but instead it transforms into something else or transfers to somewhere else. Into what or where, however, cannot be explained with the same method—even with modern science. We do not cease to live when we leave this physical life; rather, we transform into our true essence (that of the spirit) and return to our true home within the spirit world.

Looking back, I can see how every experience brought me to the knowledge and understanding I have today. In this book I share some of these remarkable experiences, which are taken from real life and real people alive in both the physical and spiritual worlds. If I had not lived to experience them myself, I am not sure if I would truly believe.

Yet through my life's journey I have learned about the spirit world; about spirit communication, spirit guides, angels, animal totems, and reincarnation. Most rewarding of all, I have rediscovered my lost Indigenous culture and the language of spirit. The language of spirit is a universal language which transcends all spoken languages, on this planet and every planet in the universe.

I never took a class in this language; I never took a course on spirituality. Rather, it is something that just happened to me, and I feel as though this was my true calling all my life—made, perhaps, as a soul contract before my current incarnation as Shawn Leonard. Perhaps I was chosen in this way to help people come to a new understanding of the spiritual world.

I have trouble calling this knowledge and understanding a gift, as so many people refer to it. I like to tell people I know another language, and that I am a spirit translator. I truly feel blessed to have had these experiences, which have helped form my ever-changing reality.

My intention with writing and sharing these experiences is to help you see the world as I do, as not everybody has the same insight into the spiritual realm. Every day, through my readings, my live shows, and my encounters with the spirit world, I continue to learn.

In sharing my story, wisdom, and knowledge, I hope it will help you change how you see the physical and spiritual worlds. Shifting your perspective in such a way will allow you to encounter these great gifts in your own life; you will encounter the spirit world with new eyes. You will have the wisdom, and vision, to know our creator resides in us all. You will gain the ability to see, feel, hear, and know the spirit within yourself.

I firmly believe we are made of the visible and invisible universe; the Great Spirit our creator. Almost 99 per cent of the mass of the human body is comprised of six elements: oxygen, carbon, hydrogen, nitrogen, calcium, and phosphorus. If you break down every particle there isn't anything solid—just energy vibrating at your ever-changing frequency.

This means we become a new creation, every moment, on a cellular level; we become a new creation on a spiritual level with every new experience. Yet we all exist in this world as conscious, living human beings. We couldn't have consciousness if it wasn't abundant in the universe and if it wasn't due to the fact we are all part of, and made from, it.

You were surrounded by our creator's loving energy before your conceived incarnation, and in what you perceive as your present earthly form. Rather, it is your spirit and soul that are your true form, meaning you have never been separated from our creator, nor the greater consciousness of all spirits.

Each and every single person on this earth is equally important, and as we evolve our creator evolves alongside through our experiences—through this life and every life we live. The experience of our creator is not limited to just humans, but extends to everything in our world and to every planet in the universe.

We cannot be separated from that which resides within, or from that which is all around us. It is the bond of love from our creator which binds us all. When we love our family, our friends, our pets, or our planet—when we admire the vastness and greatness of the universe—we are loving and honouring our creator. We are all one!

Even if you feel separate from the people or animals you loved who are now within the spirit world, remember this is also an illusion. Allow me to help you understand how they are still with you, and how they still communicate with you.

I am glad the Great Spirit, our creator, found a way to guide you to my book. I pray my experiences, my story, and my knowledge enlightens you and give you a new understanding of both the spirit world and spirit communication.

Wela'lin (Thank you)

Enjoy, and share in my wisdom with love.

Shawn Leonard

CHAPTER 1

I Needed to Forget

To an outsider, my early life may have appeared perfectly "normal", yet my childhood was filled with extraordinary experiences. These amazing events paved the way to who I am now—what I call a "spirit talker" and what others call a medium. This life I consider to be my destiny.

I'm forever grateful to my mother, who, although a devout Catholic, also had a strong belief in the afterlife and spirit's ability to communicate with those still living. When I was five, my great-grandparents, both recently deceased, appeared in my room late one night to talk to me, she assured me this was normal and people who had just died often drop by and visit. When she heard my imaginary friend, Sam, had some controversial things to say she merely said, "Well, Sam and I don't agree." When she found out I could leave my body at night and fly around the neighbourhood her response was "Just make sure you come back in the morning!"

Although these events helped make me who I am today, there was a long period of time when I didn't even remember I had experienced them—that's how successful I became at "putting them away." I now consider these moments all clues as to my life path, but it certainly wasn't clear to me then. In fact, as I got older it was as though I placed many of the more interesting events from my childhood in a sealed box, placed it in a closet, and forgot. So, for a long time, when people asked about my early life, I would say it was just a normal upbringing for a typical country boy from Nova Scotia. Two parents who were happily enough married, and a younger brother.

The only so-called "odd" thing about our family was the fact we were outsiders. Most of those living in the rural area of Elmsdale, Nova Scotia (where we lived), had been born-and-raised there. In contrast, my mother grew up in Newfoundland, one in a large, close-knit family of sixteen children. My father was from Alberta, but was stationed in Nova Scotia when he joined the navy out of high school. By then, my mother had moved, and was working her first job at Moir's Chocolate Factory. They met at a roller skating rink in Halifax. My father pretended he couldn't skate, banged into my mother, and asked her out. The rest, as they say, is history!

My parents chose to settle in Elmsdale because it was outside the busy city, and was known for its lumber mills (but not much else). The only store close by was a mile away from our house. As a kid I spent a lot of time on my bike, riding around the countryside. Sometimes I played with friends, but I was often alone, wandering through the backwoods, up to sixteen kilometres from home. I came in to eat, sleep, and go to church on Sundays (something my mother made me do!).

As my dad had a military job, he was often away for up to six months at a time. During his absences my mother kept the house running, and also made time to explore the outdoors with me and my brother. I remember many days spent swimming in the river, picking berries, and taking long walks. When my dad returned from sea we would fish and hunt. He was a trained sharpshooter and would try to teach me his tricks, but I was never very good with a gun.

My father also liked to drink a few beers, and had the belly to prove it. He also smoked, and I remember having many conversations with him about getting healthy and taking better care of himself.

Every Christmas, and every summer, my whole family would travel to Fortune Bay, Newfoundland, to visit my grandmother. My mother's siblings had happily welcomed my father into the fold, and loved us kids dearly. My brother and I always had a ball, playing with our cousins and doing a lot of fishing.

That large Newfoundland family lost two of its elders when I was still quite young. My great-grandparents, Richard and Agnes Stewart, passed in close proximity to each other and, to my surprise, took up a nightly residence in *my* bedroom! I remember waking up, around two in the morning, and seeing their shadowy figures moving about the room, whispering to each other. As mentioned, when I told my mom about it she assured me this was completely normal, and said they were visiting because they loved me. This went on for some time, and the sound of their voices often woke me up. I would lie there with my eyes shut, straining to hear what they were saying.

One such night I felt a hand running its fingers through my hair. I assumed it was my mom, thinking she had perhaps snuck in to check on me, but when I opened my eyes no one was there. The lights were off and the door was shut. I did a backflip off my bed and was in my mom's room before my feet touched the floor. The talking was one thing, but touching was quite another. I didn't like it. I told my mother they had to go, so she suggested I simply ask them to leave. The next night, before falling asleep, I talked to them out loud, pleading with them to not to visit anymore. They listened, and I didn't have contact with either of them until a certain day a couple of decades later. (But that's a story for another chapter!)

There was another spiritual figure from my childhood; one who never frightened me and who I never wanted to send away. His name was Sam, and he was what adults often refer to as an imaginary friend. Except Sam wasn't imaginary! Up to the time I was five he was my constant companion, joining me as I played—especially when alone. Sam was probably in his late twenties or early thirties, and was about six feet tall with dirty blond hair and piercing blue eyes. Although he seemed very "flesh and blood" to me, Sam was one of my spirit guides. In fact, he still is.

Sam and I would talk about all kinds of things, including some fairly controversial topics I would later report to my mother and which sometimes caused alarm. One such time was when Sam told me about the woman in the painting of *The Last Supper*. That's right—a woman! Sam said the person sitting next to Jesus in the picture was named Mary Magdalene and she was actually married to Jesus. "People won't believe you when you tell them this," said Sam, "but one day they'll find out it's true." Sam was right. Not only did my mother not believe me she tried to convince me the figure was just an effeminate John, the apostle, insisting Jesus had never been married and my friend Sam didn't know what he was talking about.

Sam was someone I could see, hear, and even feel. He used to grab my hand, and sometimes playfully shove me. He was as real to me as any other living person, so when he completely disappeared it was a pretty traumatic thing for someone so young.

The day he left was an ordinary day. I was down in the basement, playing with my dinky cars by the washing machine. Sam was with me, like he always was, but I remember him telling me he had to go. "Shawn," he said, "I have to leave, but I want you to know I'm always going to be with you, even though you won't be able to see me anymore."

I didn't know what he was talking about. For as long as I could remember, Sam had always been there and I couldn't imagine life without him. He went on, saying, "I'll always be with you. If you ever need me, just talk to me." There was a big flash of the whitest light I had ever seen—and he was gone. Sam had completely vanished.

I suddenly felt so alone; in a way I never had up to that point, and in a way that felt completely wrong. I remember crying and crying all day. I tried to talk to my friend, but wasn't able to see or hear him anymore. He had always been with me, and then suddenly wasn't. It felt like my best friend had died. It was devastating.

A couple of years later I again had a direct experience with Sam. It was not in a physical form this time, but in a way that made me understand he really was still with me like he had promised. I was just learning to ride a bike and was being reckless, doing those crazy things kids do—like setting up ramps on steep hills! As I was barreling down one such hill I hit the ramp the wrong way and went flying through the air. In the moment between my body leaving my bike and the ensuing impact, I realized it was going to be a nasty one. I suddenly felt my body being grabbed and turned upright, so instead of landing on my head I landed on my feet, and wasn't injured at all. The other kids were in awe, as was I. To them it looked like a supernatural miracle, but I knew it was Sam.

Although my spirit guide no longer appeared in physical form past the age of five, there were other magical things I was able to hold onto a little longer. The ability to leave my body at night and fly through my town was one of them. We've all had dreams of flying, but this was different. For one thing, it happened like clockwork: every night, in that strange state between being awake and being asleep. For another, my town looked ever-so-slightly different. There was always a dusky half-light I have come to think of as the light of the astral world, which is closely layered on top of our own, and to which, as a child, I had direct access.

Every night it was the same thing. I would be falling asleep when I'd suddenly find myself standing in front of my house, drenched in this sunset light, before quickly lifting off the ground. I'd then make up my mind as to which direction I wanted to go, and then off I'd fly, zipping through the sky. The topography was exactly the same, and so was the placement of all the houses. The only thing different was there were never any people in this dusk world. Never, that is, but for one exception.

On that occasion I saw an older woman, wearing a long, dark Victorian-style dress, floating over the telephone poles. She had an umbrella like Mary Poppins, and looked as though she was straight out of the 1800s. When I tried to talk to her she just looked at me, stuck up her nose, and floated on by. Excited by her presence, there was another person whom I looked for in this dusk world, yet never found. His name was David and he was a classmate who died of leukemia when I was about six years old. When he passed I told my mom I was going to use my nighttime flights to find him. That evening I flew to his house, but no one was there. When I awoke the next morning I told my mom I hadn't been able to find him, and she assured me this was because he was now in heaven.

These two experiences—seeing the woman dressed in period clothing, and being unable to find David—helped form my beliefs about the astral world. I believe it is a place of lower vibration, where spirits who haven't fully embraced the light still reside. It is a place which exists between our realities here on earth and those in the spirit world.

I had these nighttime adventures until I was about eight or nine years old, and can clearly remember realizing my ability to fly was leaving me. I would fall asleep and still appear outside my house, but I would remain earth-bound. I recall flapping my arms, thinking it would help. I actually got a bit of lift off that way, and a couple of times I even reached the height of the telephone poles. Yet I'd quickly float back down. At some point I became unable to leave the ground at all, and I remember feeling sad I could no longer fly.

Little did I know that my nighttime flights, the visits from my great-grandparents, and my conversations with Sam were just a taste of what was to come.

But first, in order to remember, I had to forget.

CHAPTER 2

The Dark and the Light

And forget I did.

By the time I was fifteen, anything not connected to the reality of my daily life was ancient history. Brushes with the spirit world had been replaced by crushes on girls, practising the guitar, and starting to learn things about being an adult.

My dad was one of my biggest teachers in this respect. When his ship docked and he returned home, he would always involve me in whatever projects he had on the go. Sometimes it was hunting, while others it was jobs around the house. He was very intelligent and really good with anything mechanical. One winter he took the motor out of his car (a Chevrolet Nova SS) and brought it inside the house because we didn't have a garage. He then took the entire motor apart, piece by piece, and put it back together—just for fun! He also taught himself guitar, and would let me watch and ask as many questions I liked.

With twenty-two years of military service behind him, my dad was due to retire in only three years. He told me he was sick of travelling and being away from his family for such long periods. His plan was to continue to work to bring in money, while still having his pension supplement our family's income. I remember him taking me out to the airport and showing me a new company called Pratt & Whitney. He was taking courses that would help him get a job there as a mechanic.

In the fall of 1987, my dad was building a garage so he could tinker with his vehicles outside during the winter. On Saturday, October 14, we had just finished framing the structure and were waiting for the cement to be poured. We were taking a break in the kitchen, having a glass of water, when I noticed how much my dad was sweating. I chalked it up to hard work, but then he told me he had a really bad cramp in his hand and wondered aloud if he should be worried. I told him I didn't know, but that maybe he should quit smoking and go see the doctor. He had smoked cigarettes for as long as I could remember, and although there were times he told my mom he'd quit, I would catch him smoking in the basement by the wood stove. He also liked to have a few beers with his navy buddies, and so carried a bit of extra weight. My mom and I were always bugging him about getting healthier, and this time was no different.

Then, on Monday, October 16, I woke up to my mom yelling for help. "There's something wrong with your dad. He's out in the driveway. His truck is running but I can't wake him up." I ran outside, past his truck with the door hanging open, and to the end of the driveway. He wasn't there. I ran back into the house and told my mom I couldn't see him anywhere. She grabbed my hand and dragged me back down the driveway. There he was; laying on the ground beside the truck. When

I realized he wasn't breathing, I tried to remember all I had learned in Scouts about CPR.

In an emergency, time does funny things. The few short minutes during which I tried to resuscitate my father seemed to pass very slowly. Questioning whether I had the number of chest compressions correct, I attempted to breathe life back into him, to no avail. I remember screaming at him, telling his spirit to get back into his body and return to us. I also plead with God. Suddenly there were neighbours present and I was walking into the house to tell my mom that Dad wasn't coming back.

He was only forty-two. The fact that I ran right past where he lay in the driveway, but didn't see him, will always be a mystery to me. Perhaps I wasn't ready for the harsh reality of my father being gone, and doing so was some kind of protective mechanism. Or maybe I was just in deep shock.

I don't remember much about the days that followed. I know my mom's large Newfoundland family descended on our house, and there were many meals delivered to our door. I know my friends stopped by. And I know that sense of unreality continued. I did not want what happened to be true, and found it very hard to focus. In fact, I failed ninth grade that year because although I would go to school I wasn't really present. Needless to say, it was a very tough time.

My gift that first Christmas without him was a guitar. Seeing I had enjoyed watching and learning from him, my dad bought me my own guitar. He hid it in his bunk on the ship, knowing if it was at home I would find it and ruin the surprise. It still wasn't fully paid off when he died, but my dad's navy buddies took care of that bill. They also sent my mom a card with some extra money to help her out. But they did change one thing: rather than send me the new guitar, never strummed, they sent my dad's well-loved instrument, which I treasured.

Over the next year, I did the same things other sixteen-year-olds do: listened to loud music, grew my hair long, joined a band, smoked some weed, and stayed out too late. My mother would get mad at me for not coming home on time and sneaking in and out of the house. One October night, almost a year since my dad had passed, I was out late. Not wanting to wake my mother up I decided to sleep on the couch in the basement. Soon after I fell asleep I woke up, only to find myself outside my body, looking down at myself sleeping on the couch. It was a similar feeling to my childhood flying dreams, in that I was hyper-alert and very aware something unusual was happening.

Suddenly, an enormous white light appeared in the middle of the room. It was the largest, brightest light I had ever seen, and reminded me of the white flash when Sam disappeared from my life. But this light was even brighter and larger, and it lasted for longer than an instant. This light stayed. Then, to my great surprise and delight, my father walked out of that big, beautiful doorway.

He looked fantastic: incredibly healthy and smiling broadly, but without his trademark eyeglasses. He was wearing a white robe, similar to the one Sam had worn. My father emanated tremendous love and joy as he looked at me, and the word "glistening" came to my mind as I smiled back. He was just so vibrant.

"Oh my God, Dad!" The moment the words were out of my mouth I went quickly from elation to anger, asking why the hell he'd left us. I told him how bad things had been since he died, how Mom was struggling to pay off the mortgage. "I hardly saw you because you were gone all the time, and then you had to friggin *die*? It's not fair."

My dad just smiled and told me to calm down. "I have some things to tell you, Shawn. There are a few things you need to know," he said. "The first thing is that I'm okay and I'm in a good place. You need to tell your mom and your brother that I love them and I'm watching over them."

He continued talking, and as he did I looked behind him into the light. I could see ornate, white marble pillars and stairs. "You're not going to understand this right now," he said, "but everything happens for a reason. This was my time to leave, and that was the plan before you or I were even born. It was my time to go home."

As if that weren't enough information, he went on. "I want you to remember this light; this light is everything. You're going to help people know this, and you're going to help them understand why we're here and where we go after we die."

This bit of information stopped me in my tracks. "What are you talking about?" I asked.

"I know this doesn't make sense now, but it will," he said.

I was completely bewildered. "What do you mean I'm going to help people? How the hell am I supposed to do that?"

Again he smiled at me, full of love. "Don't worry. When the time comes, Shawn, you won't have to do anything! It'll just be something that happens. You'll know what I mean when it does."

Then, as if sensing my inability to comprehend what he was saying, he changed the subject and actually told a joke. A stupid joke. I can't remember the punchline, but I do remember him laughing and laughing. As our conversation shifted, I became rather entranced by the world behind my father, the one from which he had so suddenly appeared. I was mostly fixated on the alluring, magnificent light, and the way it felt. There was something about it that felt like home, and I found myself wanting to see more of the world where my father now was; I wanted to experience the feeling of walking into that light.

As if reading my mind, my father suddenly turned serious. "Shawn, you can look, but I can't let you come here."

"Why not?" I asked. "I promise I'll come right back."

He then informed me that if I walked into the light I would want to stay. As he was saying this, I strongly felt the so-called "realness" of the place waiting behind my father. This is hard to explain, because to most of us our world feels so real and solid, but as I looked and compared the two it was as if our world paled and shrunk in comparison to what lay beyond. I wanted so badly to experience it for myself. I even tried to sneak past him, but he intercepted me with a light touch to the middle of my forehead "Shawn, just remember what I said."

I was suddenly back in my body, on the couch. I lay there for a long time, looking at the space where he had appeared, willing both my father and the light to return.

But they never did.

CHAPTER 3

Farewell to Nova Scotia

It was incredibly soothing to see my father again, especially to see him looking so well and happy. When I told my mother the next morning she wasn't as relieved as I thought she'd be, and was perhaps a little cheesed off my dad had visited me and not her. Whether or not she appreciated what had happened, the experience stayed with me—something incredibly real and amazing. The part about my dad telling me I would help people was mystifying, however, I soon forgot about it. It just didn't make sense. Simply knowing my dad still loved me and watched over me somehow secured me to my life again. It was then things began to shift.

I made a couple of new friends who weren't as into smoking marijuana as the rest of the high school crowd. I started playing guitar, in earnest this time. I also started dating someone, and it lasted longer than the one-month "relationships" I'd been in before. Her name was Ashley, and for the first time in my life I felt as though I'd fallen in love.

My grades improved and my friends and I graduated. Suddenly we all needed to decide what we were doing with our lives. One of my friends started driving a truck, another went off to university, and Ashley joined the military. I didn't know what I wanted to do, but if I were to stay in Elmsdale the options were limited. There was the grocery store, the gas station, or the lumber mill. As someone who enjoyed being outside and doing physical labour, working at the lumber mill seemed the best option.

Getting the job wasn't as easy as I thought, and I had to go back every day for two weeks before they finally agreed to hire me. I had no idea what I was getting myself into. It was back-breaking work, and the guys I worked with were a bit rough. They were also hard on the young new guy, pushing the lumber through the saw at a pace destined to break anyone. If you survived a week you weren't too bad, and if you survived two, well, that was something. I lasted one month; just long enough for me to do the math and figure out that the most money I would ever make at the lumber mill was about fourteen dollars an hour. That would never be enough to support a family.

I still didn't know what I wanted to do for a living, but I knew I could probably work at almost anything I put my mind to. My plan was to wait and see where Ashley was posted, and then leave Elmsdale to be with her. I'd find work wherever we landed. The only problem with that plan was when Ashley came back from boot camp she told me she wanted to see other people. Before I could even blink there was a guy in a uniform sitting at her kitchen table, talking to her parents; the same place I'd been just a few short months before.

It was a real blow. And it meant I had to re-evaluate where I was going, and what I had thought my life would look like.

Enter my Newfoundland grandmother. She happened to call just around the time Ashley broke my heart, and told me my Uncle Sam was looking for a fishing partner. Having loved spending summers with this part of my family I was quick to say yes, and I spent the next year living the life of a fisherman while doing a little bit of dating; just enough to make me feel as though I was starting to heal from the break-up with Ashley.

That year I also spent a lot of time with my grandmother. One of the things I grew up knowing, but didn't think about a lot, was the fact my grandmother had grown-up in the Native community of Conne River. She is Mi'kmaq, but left her community to marry my grandfather. Sometimes we would visit the place she grew up—located right across the bay—but for the most part our Mi'kmaq heritage wasn't something we really acknowledged nor talked about.

During my time in Newfoundland, all of that changed. My grandmother and I would stay up playing cards. She would weave in stories of her family and the years she spent growing up, smoking the whole time she spoke. Her grandmother had been a medicine woman, so she was privy to all kinds of healing remedies most people would dismiss as nonsense—but I've seen them work!

One of the most important, and surprising, things I learned about my grandmother was that she could definitely see and feel and hear things other people couldn't. It wasn't unusual for her to be washing the dishes at the kitchen sink, only to suddenly grab the broom and run outside. I would watch her chase something through the yard (something I couldn't see!) while yelling and brandishing the broom. She would return, out of breath, yet triumphant. "There was a bad spirit out there," she would say. "I chased it away!"

At the time, I didn't know whether or not to think she was crazy, or to believe she really could see something real. Of course, I know now we share the same gift: that of being in touch with spirit.

In other supernatural territory, Newfoundland offered first exposure to Ouija boards. My Aunt Darlene would gather friends for "spooky" evenings at a remote location right on the ocean. We'd light candles and ask questions of "the dead". Mostly, we'd have a good laugh. Yet there were a couple of things that happened which made Aunt Darlene stop the Ouija sessions and call me "crazy".

The first was when I told them about the flashes I saw of a young man who had died nearby, detailed enough to know what he looked like and what he was doing when he died. It ended up being accurate. The other was as we sat around the circle I would watch the faces of my friends, lit up by the candlelight, and watch their faces melt and transform, before my eyes, into hundreds of other faces. Black, white, Asian; women, men, children. I found it fascinating, but when I asked if the others could see it too—thinking it was a trick of the light—the room became eerily still. That didn't happen for other people.

Again, I tucked these experiences away and focused on fishing, family, and dating casually. My wounded heart was slowly healing—or so it felt until I got an unexpected phone call.

"Shawn? It's Ashley." She was crying hard, and my heart was suddenly pounding in my throat.

"Oh my God. Ashley? What's wrong? Are you okay?"

"I'm so sorry, Shawn. I made some big mistakes."

Was this an apology call? For breaking up with me?

"You're the best thing that ever happened to me. Did you know that?" She continued, still crying as she talked. "I really regret breaking up with you."

I held my breath during the long pause that followed.

"Do you think we can get back together and make it work?"

I exhaled. My broken heart was lapping up all her words, completely shutting off my rational brain. "Where are you?" I asked.

"I'm in Ottawa."

"Okay. I'll come to you. Just give me a few days to figure out how to get there."

I don't remember if she said "thanks" or "I love you" or even "goodbye". All I knew was that I was packing my bags and leaving Newfoundland. I was heading off to be with the girl I loved, and all was right with the world.

Until it wasn't.

Back in Nova Scotia a few days later, I got a phone call from Ashley saying she'd been confused and lonely the night she called, and hadn't meant what she said. She wished me well, but said in no uncertain terms she didn't want me to come to Ottawa. She didn't want to get back together. Period. I was nineteen years old, without any sense of a path or a purpose. I was again adrift.

Once more, my mother's family stepped in. This time it was my mom's youngest sister, who lived in Calgary, Alberta. She was dating a guy who worked for an office-furniture company. It was growing fast and he was in need of some new workers. I weighed my options: stay in Nova Scotia and work at the lumber mill, or go back to Newfoundland. Or try something completely different.

I opted for different. Calgary seemed a big, exciting city, and I was more than ready for something new. I packed a bag and my guitar, and bought a one-way ticket to Calgary. I had a place to stay, two hundred dollars in my wallet, and the prospect of work on the horizon.

I took a deep breath, said goodbye to Nova Scotia, and flew off into a whole new chapter of my life. One that would open a door to my future self; the self I was surprised to find waiting for me.

CHAPTER 4

Hello Alberta

Only a week into my new life in Calgary, I had a job at the office-furniture company in the metal fabrication department. Shortly thereafter, I went to a Canada Day concert with a friend, and met the woman I would end up marrying—Marissa. Real life was happening quickly now. It was like I stepped onto the conveyer belt called Being an Adult, and was being swiftly carried off into a whole new land. A land full of very grown-up experiences indeed.

After two years of dating, Marissa got pregnant, and we decided to get married before the baby was born. I quickly moved into a permanent position within the company, in the wood department, building custom office furniture. I was good at it and I enjoyed it; and felt as though I'd finally found my niche.

Then, on a visit to the doctor I got some disturbing news.

I had been thinking a lot about my dad, and how he'd died so young, so I decided to get checked out and set my mind at ease. That didn't happen! The doctor told me I had potentially life-threatening cholesterol levels, and warned me if I didn't change my lifestyle—stop smoking, exercise more, and eat better—he would have to put me on heart pills. I was twenty-one years old! It was a huge wake-up call. I was so scared I virtually changed my life overnight. I went from being a mostly sedentary guy (when I wasn't at work) to a gym- and exercise- fanatic. I also stopped smoking and eating junk food, and within three months had completely turned my health around.

When I think about what happened next I marvel at how the Great Spirit waited until my life had settled and I had achieved some stability—a family, a good job, and my health—before it pulled out all the stops and really started to show me my soul's purpose. And it started at a Tim Horton's, of all places.

I had a friend named Jimmy, who worked at the Tim Horton's, and after picking up the baby from the sitter I'd go and meet him after work for coffee. While we worked, the coffee shops hustle and bustle all around us, I would start to recognize the faces of the people he worked with every day. Slowly, I realized I would get a feeling, a sort of knowing, about certain people. There was one guy whom I thought was stealing from the till. I never saw anything odd, it was just a feeling I had. I felt the same with another guy I suspected was dealing drugs. Then the same with two other employees, both married to other people, whom I became convinced were having an affair. I would ask Jimmy what he thought about my suspicions, and he was appalled! He thought I was crazy and would say things like "Why do you think that?" or "Why would you say something like that?" or "That's not happening!"

To my surprise, within a one-week period I had heard from Jimmy, the first guy got caught stealing and was fired.

The second guy got arrested and thrown in jail for dealing drugs. My friend actually caught the couple I suspected were having an affair kissing in the back room. I remember Jimmy coming to my home and telling me what had happened, asking incredulously "How did you know that?"

I told him what I thought was true: that it was just a vibe I picked up on, and that everyone could do it. Jimmy didn't agree. He thought it was something more and confided in a few of his friends about what happened. One of his friends, Amber, was a self-confessed psychic junkie, and when she heard the story asked Jimmy if I could "read" her. I didn't even really know what that meant!

"She just wants to see what you can get about her just from reading her vibe. Like you did at my work."

The whole idea made me nervous. I had no idea what I would say or what "reading" someone entailed. I didn't know what I was doing! My friend reassured me, saying I should just tell Amber whatever popped into my head.

The night arrived and Amber came over to my house. I was still nervous, but after what had happened at the restaurant I was also curious as to what I could (if anything) pick up from someone I didn't know. This was a living experiment, right in front of me on the couch. I didn't know a thing about Amber except that she worked with Jimmy. So, I just went with it.

"I think you're going to meet a guy named Don, and it's a romantic thing. You'll be interested in each other."

"I just met a guy named Don." Being a so-called "psychic junkie", Amber didn't look as surprised as I felt. *I can't believe I got a name right*, I thought to myself. *How did I do that?* I went on. "I have a feeling you're a writer, and you're going to write a book."

"Well, I am working on a book."

My stomach was doing flip-flops. Was this real? Or was I just really good at guessing? "And I feel like you'll be travelling around the world, but in a different way. Staying in people's homes. And I'm seeing a lot of animals."

Amber then told me and Jimmy about her plan to do the accounting for her father's business, but to do it remotely. "I have this dream of seeing the world, and working from various places, by taking care of other people's houses and their pets. Is that really going to happen?" Amber was excited; and so was I. She then cut right to the chase.

"Can you connect with someone in the spirit world?" She was sitting on the edge of the couch now, staring at me intently.

"What?" I wasn't sure I'd heard her correctly.

"Someone in the spirit world. Someone who's died?"

I had heard her right. "I don't think so. I don't know? I've never done that before."

"Can you try? There's someone who I've always wanted to connect with."

"Um, I'm pretty sure I don't know how to do that. But, yes, I'll try." It seemed so important. I didn't want to disappoint.

I stared at the wall behind the couch and my logical brain kicked in. I tried to focus by concentrating on the fact she wanted a message from her grandmother—or someone like that. I waited to get a feeling, or an image of an older woman. But what came surprised me. I saw a teenaged boy, standing in what looked like a suburban backyard, dressed in a baseball uniform. He was looking at me while tossing a ball up and down in one hand. He did that for a while, then turned and walked into the shed behind him. I had no idea why this image popped into my mind, and I was pretty positive it wasn't what she was looking for. "I saw something ... but it's weird. It's probably right out to lunch and not relevant at all, but...." And then I told her.

I won't ever forget the look on Amber's face, or the tears that immediately began rolling down her cheeks. "That's him," she said. "He was my best friend and we played baseball together. He was battling depression, and one night after a game he went out to his shed and took his own life."

Oh my God.

Amber continued. "I've always wanted to know if he was okay. Do you think he's alright now?"

I was trying to hide my own shock about what had just happened, while also rapidly trying to process and understand it. My first thought was *I must be a mind reader.* I must have simply read her thoughts. She was thinking about him and somehow I picked that up.

Amber interrupted my inner turmoil. "Shawn, is he okay? Is he happy?"

I didn't know! But I sensed how important this was to her. "This is all new to me. I really don't know how he is now, but I'm sure he's okay."

When Amber left my house that night she was really happy. So happy, in fact, she went to work and told all her co-workers. Then she went out with her friends and told all of them. She told her family, too. I started getting phone calls. Turned out lots of people wanted to set up a time to meet with me; people who wanted me to "read" them, and others who wanted to connect with loved ones who had died.

What the hell? I thought. What was going on? How was all this happening? In the days after my time with Amber my mind was reeled and shut doors all over the place. There was no way dead people were communicating with me. No way! That particular option could not be true because that was far too out there.

Boy, was I in for a surprise.

CHAPTER 5

Spirit Talks

From nine to five, every day, my life looked just as it used to. Yet in my down-time, after work and on weekends, things were suddenly very different and very interesting. I received so many phone calls, and so much interest in my readings, that a few weeks after the exciting first reading with Amber I was already booked solid for three months. I wasn't doing it every day, and I certainly hadn't yet embraced it fully, but there was no doubt people were getting something out of the readings.

All the while, I kept asking myself how this was happening. I was a guy who worked for a company that manufactured office furniture. I had never taken a class, nor had any training, and I didn't know much about spiritual things. Simply put, I was confused. Was I a mind reader? Was I able to pick up on people's thoughts and their memories of those who had passed on? Is that what this gift was?

I kept expecting I would wake-up; that my life would return to the way it used to be. But that didn't happen. This was real. As that slowly dawned upon me—that this thing I never expected was now a big part of my life—I decided to be as open as possible and learn as much as I could.

It was a rich time with a lot of new experiences flooding in; some of which took some time getting used to. At night, just before drifting off to sleep, I began to see faces. These weren't faces of people I knew. Rather, it was like a rolodex of random faces, flashing one after the other in quick succession. African, Asian, Caucasian, Indigenous; elderly, middle-aged, children, babies. A wide variety of faces, looked right at me, and in a constant flow. I couldn't get to sleep each night without first seeing what felt like a thousand faces.

During the day, I felt as though my intuition was increasingly spot on. I would have flashes of insight, instances of just knowing something, only to then have it confirmed. Movies and TV shows were now predictable and boring, as I always knew who the bad guy was, how the mystery would be solved, or how the story would end. Marissa didn't like going to the movies with me because I always wrecked the ending!

This knowing bled into my work life, and one instance early on surprised me. It was astonishing the accuracy of the kind of truth I was privy to—without even understanding from where the information was coming.

Sean was a new guy in my department. He was a big, burly fellow who looked like a football player. One day, when he walked by me, in my mind's eye I could see him buying a pony. It seemed ludicrous and impossible that a huge, husky man like Sean would want to buy a pony! But the image was persistent and wouldn't let me go. As I was trying to be open to whatever knowing came in I decided to ask him about it.

"Sean," I said, walking up to his desk. "I have a really weird question to ask you, and you're probably going to think this is completely silly, but here goes! Are you planning on buying a pony?"

Dead silence. He just stared at me, looking shocked. "How the hell did you know that?"

Turns out, just an hour before, Sean was on Kijiji looking for a pony for his daughter. He and his wife owned some land outside Calgary, and had been talking about getting a horse but felt their young daughter was too small. So they had changed their minds and decided on a pony. "I was just going to call the guy and arrange to go see it," he said, still staring at me hard and trying to figure out what in the world was going on. I could see the wheels turning in his mind, and could see the questions forming. Sean was wondering if I had somehow tapped into his computer and accessed browser history.

I had actually shocked myself. What I had picked up was so specific, and so accurate, and it had come out of nowhere. It acted like a big checkmark next to the idea of myself as a mind reader; someone who could tune into people's energy if they were in the vicinity. Then something happened to radically shift that idea.

One of my long-time co-workers was a man named Orhan. We had become friends, often playing sports like basketball and soccer together. During this period of my life, when things were growing ever more bizarre, I would confide in Orhan about the new abilities I seemed to have acquired. He would mostly scoff. In retrospect, I understand that at the time I needed Orhan's logical way of seeing the world, as well as his down-to-earth nature to keep me grounded. There were moments when I feared I was going crazy, but somehow Orhan's skepticism about all I was experiencing kept one foot in the so-called real world—something I needed as my reality morphed.

Orhan and I sat side by side at work. One day, while at our desks, I heard a name in my head, as if on repeat. The name was Charlie. It felt like a voice separate from my own, as if someone was whispering to me through my mind; it was very different from having a thought of my own. The experience continued for nearly an hour, and in addition to being persistent and distracting it was also a little scary. I started thinking that maybe there was something wrong with my brain, that there was some mental health issue at play, and said to myself, *Great, I'm schizophrenic*. I wondered if maybe I needed to go to a doctor, one who could help me. At the very least, it felt like I might need to go home sick for the rest of the day.

I turned to Orhan to tell him that I wasn't feeling well and was going to head home. When I looked at my friend the voice stopped. I looked away, back at my computer, when it started again. I looked back at Orhan and it stopped. I was still freaked out, but now a little relieved. *This must be the mind reader thing*, I thought. *Orhan must be thinking about a friend named Charlie, and that's what I'm picking up.*

I had to know, however, and braced myself for Orhan's disbelief. "Orhan, I know you already think I'm crazy, but I have to ask you something."

He rolled his eyes and sighed, keeping his face turned toward his computer screen. "What now?"

"Do you know a guy named Charlie?"

Slowly, Orhan turned toward me. "Why do you ask that?"

There was something about the way he spoke that sent a quick chill through my spine. I didn't know what nerve I'd hit, but I had definitely hit one. "The name Charlie just keeps popping in my head," I said. "You must be thinking about him?"

"I'm not thinking about him right now. But I was thinking about him a couple of weeks ago. He's someone I used to work with at the airport, around eight years ago."

As soon as Orhan said that I got an image of a sign for a local bar in Calgary. It was called the T&C, for Town and

Country. "Why am I seeing the sign for the T&C now?" I said this mostly to myself, but Orhan overheard.

"What did you say?" he asked, but this time his whole body tensed and his eyes locked onto mine. "I'm pretty sure that was the last place Charlie was seen alive."

It was as if all the air had suddenly been sucked out of my lungs, and I shivered with intense goosebumps. "Are you shitting me? You're not serious?" What was Orhan saying? The T&C was the last place Charlie was seen alive. *Does that mean he's now dead?* Why would I be getting an image of the last place this guy Charlie—who I didn't even know—was last seen?

"Is he dead? Is Charlie dead?"

"Yeah. He was murdered."

"What?" Orhan narrowed his eyes. "Who have you been talking to?"

Oh my God. He thought I was playing a terrible trick! "Nobody! I swear. I just heard this guy's name and then saw the T&C sign in my head."

Orhan was really angry. "This isn't nice. You shouldn't do this to people."

Just then another image came. It felt as though I was standing at the top of a set of stairs and there were people all around me, and then I was walking down the stairs. Down the stairs, over and over. "And now I'm seeing stairs, someone going down a flight of stairs." I was so shocked by these sudden and vivid images I couldn't help speaking them out loud. "And you're not thinking any of these things I'm seeing?" I was completely bewildered.

"No! I wasn't thinking about Charlie or the Town and Country or stairs. I don't know what you're talking about." Orhan stopped, suddenly realizing his voice had got too loud. "Have you been talking to someone I used to work with?" he whispered.

I was still reeling from the last image, and it took a moment to realize Orhan was accusing me of being some sort of con artist. "I haven't talked to anyone. I didn't even know you worked at the airport, so how could I know who you worked with? Are you sure you weren't just thinking about Charlie?"

"I don't know what you're doing, but I don't like this at all. Just stop it." Orhan turned his whole body around and faced his computer, mad as hell.

My mind was in overdrive, trying to process what was happening. *If Orhan wasn't just thinking about Charlie, as he claimed he wasn't, how did Charlie's name come into my head?* This was entirely new territory. I felt as though I were desperately trying to shove all the puzzle pieces into place, but nothing fit. In the meantime, my friend was now mad at me and thought I was messing with his head.

"Listen, Orhan," I said. "I promise I'm not screwing around with you. I don't know what's going on either, but I can see you're frustrated with me so let's just drop it. I'm sorry—I didn't mean to upset you."

And so drop it we did.

I tried to get back to a regular life. At the time, in addition to working hard and raising a daughter with my wife, I was also big into fitness as a result of my health scare. I ran and went to the gym and lifted weights. There was a lot to keep me busy, including the increasing number of people who called and wanted to book a reading.

One day, about six months after the strange conversation with Orhan, I left the gym and headed to work. I stopped for a coffee, and finding I had a little extra time, I did something I usually didn't have the chance to do in those days: I picked up a newspaper.

When I got to the office I still had ten minutes before I had to work, so I sat down with my coffee and a copy of the

Calgary Sun and started flipping. Right away, an article about an unsolved murder in Calgary caught my attention. A former airport employee named Manequin Achari, but who went by Charlie, had been found dead in his basement apartment eight years previous. He was last seen at the Town and Country, and his killer was still at large. The police were still looking for information that might lead to an arrest.

I felt as though I'd been hit by a ton of bricks. When Orhan walked in a few minutes later I shoved the newspaper at him "Orhan, you need to read this!" He took it, read it, and turned to me. "Do you remember us talking about your friend Charlie?" I asked him.

He sighed. "What do you want me to say?"

"I want you to tell me you remember the part where I said the thing about the stairs. They found his body in a basement apartment!"

"Sure, I remember."

"And you didn't know anything about him living in a basement apartment, right?"

"Sure, that's right. I didn't know. Why is that so important?"

"Because if you didn't know about him living in a basement apartment then you weren't thinking about stairs, which means I am not a mind reader and that the information came from some other source."

Orhan looked dubious.

"Orhan, I really, really need you to be honest with me, and I need you to swear you're telling me the truth. Are you sure you don't know anything about where or how this guy died?"

"I swear I didn't know anything about how he died, or that he lived in a basement apartment. Okay? Are you going to leave me the hell alone now?"

Orhan could have no way of knowing it, but everything changed in that moment. If I hadn't picked up all that information from Orhan then from who, or where, was it coming? Was it possible it was coming from Charlie? Was it possible I was actually receiving communications from the spirit world?

This idea suddenly felt very real and very alive to me, and I can honestly say my life changed entirely that day. It was nothing less than an epiphany and it came with the force of a lightning bolt, illuminating everything around me. "Orhan," I said, "I think dead people are really communicating to me. This is crazy!"

In the same moment I remembered what my father's visit and what he had said to me; that I would be helping people understand why we are here, and where we go after we die. He told me I didn't have to do anything. That it would just happen.

He was right.

CHAPTER 6

Blue Jays and Dimes

After the Charlie epiphany, the floodgates opened. It was as though I had suddenly given myself permission to remember every single mystical or other-worldly experience I had ever had, but couldn't make sense of at the time. I recalled my great-grandparents visiting my room, my nighttime flights, and my friend Sam. In particular, I thought a lot about my dad visiting when I was a teenager and all the things he had said about the light.

I realized the spirit world had important and life-changing things to say to the people who were my clients. It was very humbling to know there were spirits on the other side, using me as a conduit to connect with their loved ones who showed up at my door. When people cried tears of relief or joy in my living room during a reading, because of something I had seen, I often remembered what my father had said about helping others.

It was also far more interesting than my other work. Don't get me wrong. I had a great job and I loved the people I worked with, but I felt far more passionate and experienced a deep heart connection when I did the readings. Every day was exciting and new. I couldn't wait to talk to people; I couldn't wait to see what I could envision next. It was (and still is!) a learning experience to see what new information would come into my mind—and also *how* it would make itself known.

Yet this called for a really tough balancing act. My wife and I had a second child, the business continued to grow, and I strived to find the balance between working full-time, my readings, and my family. It was hard; I had very little free time.

I also continued to struggle with charging money for the readings, especially when it came to raising my rates. I believed I should keep the "clean" spiritual realm separate from the grubbiness of money. This wasn't a new thing—I'd always had a hard time accepting payment. Somehow, it felt tainted. It took the advice of another professional medium, one who had been doing the work for a long time, to help me see the situation with more clarity. After doing a reading for her she told me I was undervaluing my own gift, falling prey to the "money isn't spiritual" belief.

She informed me the work I did was called "energy work", and that money was also energy. "This is simply an exchange for the quality of work you do," she said. "It's your time and you do it well, and you should be paid accordingly. You don't have issues paying for a piece of art or a piece of writing. It's the same thing. This is your art, and you're good at it. You need to have faith and believe the price you're asking for is fair." The medium actually encouraged me to raise my rates in an attempt to learn to value my own work, and also to solve the problem of people booking readings and then simply not showing up. I learned people who are serious are willing to pay a little bit more for their reading, *and* will keep their appointment.

Her talk gave me the courage to follow through, and it felt really good. I had less cancellations, and, in general, started to attract more serious clientele; fewer people were coming to check me out because they thought the whole thing was a flaky hoax, and more came who actually knew what they wanted out of the experience.

Another shift came when I started doing readings over the phone. It was something I had been reluctant to try, even though I knew other mediums and psychics read people this way. I wasn't sure if the energy would be the same, and I had never wanted to take that risk. But I was getting a lot of messages to just trust myself. As it turned out there was absolutely no difference in what I was able to pick up in person. In fact, one of my very first phone readings has stayed with me, in part because the client got in touch some years later, and I found out how important that reading had been.

Her name was Faye Schindelka, and she contacted me a few weeks after her brother died. She didn't tell me about her brother, but I immediately felt, and connected to, a male energy and identified it was her brother, Murray. Murray started showing me the number eleven repeatedly, and when I asked Faye why that number was important she told me he had died on November 11. Her brother was insistent this date would be important for another reason, and showed me Faye would write a book. She kindly brushed off that suggestion, saying she wrote songs and did some illustrations for books, so that must be what I was picking up.

"I don't think that's what I'm seeing," I said. "I'm seeing something different. Your brother is telling me you're going to be writing, and I think it has a lot to do with him and messages you're receiving now." Her spirit guides also came through, showing me prisms of light floating all around Faye, telling me they sent her rainbows to remind her to lighten up. I didn't know what any of that meant, but told her anyway. She laughed and responded that her whole house was filled with glass balls and prisms, and that when the sun shone there were rainbows everywhere! Murray kept nudging me to go back to the book she was going to write, yet Faye kept dismissing the notion. She wasn't rude—she just really thought I was off-track!

A few years after our reading, Faye contacted me to say she had found the notes from our call, and was amazed to see all the references to a book she would write, as well as to read how insistent her brother and I had been. She hadn't remembered what I'd said about her book, but she did indeed go on to write one! It was called *Poppies from Heaven*, and was about her continuing relationship with her brother after death; about the communication that is possible if one is open to it. The title explains why her brother informed me the number eleven would be important for another reason other than the date of his death. In Canada, Remembrance Day, one of our national holidays, is on November 11, and the custom in our country is to pin a red felt poppy to your coat.

Receiving letters and phone calls from people who were benefiting from my work felt amazing, and did a lot to build my confidence. I knew I was on the right track, and when I allowed myself to feel this way there was a sense of destiny; it was building inside me and strongly pulling me forward.

The only problem was there are only so many hours in a week, and at least forty of those went to my full-time job. Marissa was becoming increasingly unhappy with how things were unfolding, and often expressed a desire that we could have "a normal life." She told me she wished I gained a better sense of balance and wouldn't work so hard all the time. She even began to pressure me to stop doing readings.

I couldn't do that, and when I talked to her about the other option—becoming a medium full-time—she became very frightened. We had a mortgage and a car payment, and we had to feed the kids. My job paid well, and I had a benefit plan and a pension. She feared losing that kind of stability. And at the time, so did I. There was no guarantee I would continue to stay busy as a medium, and even though I strongly felt this was my calling I wasn't yet confident enough to make the leap.

None of this stopped me from continuing to build communication with the spirit world. At the time, I was meditating and praying daily—taking time to connect with my spirit guides, as well as the spirit of my father. I used to ask him for signs he was with me, and began to see three things consistently: blue jays, feathers, and dimes. To me, the dimes were a perfect representation of my father. The coin is worth ten cents, and my father died in the tenth month of the year. Also, dimes are imprinted with the image of a sailing ship (the Bluenose) on one side, which matches with the fact that my father was a sailor. Often, the dimes I found would have the year 1987 on them—the year my dad died. My father sent me so many dimes, in fact, that I started joking with him. "Dad, if you're gonna send me dimes could you send me something a little bigger? What about coins worth more, or even some dollar bills?" Apparently all I had to do was ask because that's exactly what started to happen.

It began with loonies, the Canadian one-dollar coin. The first one I found was buried in the ice of a 7-Eleven parking lot, but when I dug it out I discovered the year imprinted on it was 1987. I knew then he had heard me, and it made me wonder how much more was possible. I started to specifically ask for larger bills, and fives and tens started showing up. I remember one particular walk where the wind blew a handful of five-dollar bills at me as I was walking down the road; four of them! They blew right toward me on the breeze. The best part was a stranger helped grab them, and then handed them over like they were mine! After the twenty-dollar bills started coming I upped the ante and asked my dad for a fifty. I remember the day I found it: I was out walking in the snow when I saw something pink glistening under all the white. *Is this actually my fifty?* I thought as I bent down and brushed the snow away. It was! I truly believe when we ask the spirit world for concrete things they are overjoyed to show us how they can make things happen. I also believe they are only happy to show they can communicate in ways which are meaningful to us here on Earth.

The most amazing example of this happened while I was struggling to make ends meet. Marissa and I had just bought a bigger house in a different area of Calgary. There was a lot of work to do on the house, in both the yard and the unfinished basement, and we'd just invested a lot of cash to build a privacy fence. That was when my computer decided to die. Suddenly, I was unable to access my email to make client appointments, and I couldn't make updates to the website I had built for the business. (This was back in the day when you needed a specific program to create a web page.) A co-worker of mine, Conrad Kardash, had helped me by putting some very expensive web-authoring software on a CD. I was then able to build a website on my home computer using Conrad's CD. Once done I gave the CD back to him, and Conrad ended up leaving our company and moving somewhere else. I didn't think any more about it—until faced with the black screen of death.

I needed a new computer, and I needed it now. Biting the bullet, I went shopping and put the purchase on a credit card until I could find the money. Yet it wasn't until I got the computer home that I realized it was just an empty shell without any pre-loaded programs. I couldn't afford to buy any software. The borrowed CD was long gone, and I had no idea how to get a hold of Conrad. I turned to my current co-workers and asked if they knew how to find him; I scoured the phone book. Back then, there was no Facebook or LinkedIn to help. It felt like I had reached a dead end. So, I gave it up and I asked for help. I talked to my spirit guides and my angels, as well as any other helpful people in the spirit world, and asked them to help me find a way to connect with Conrad. And then I went on with my life.

That weekend, I needed to hang the gates on the new privacy fence. It was definitely a two-person job, so I called up my brother (who was also living in Calgary) to ask for help. He said he was going out drinking, but would be there as soon as he could the next day. We arranged for him to swing by around 10 a.m.

The next morning, I had everything measured up and prepared for his arrival. Ten o'clock came and went, and by 10:30 I knew he wasn't going to show up. I had to figure out how to do the job myself, which involved a lot of extra work. Just as I had finished and had stood back to admire the job, a car pulled up in front of my house. I heard a voice say, "Excuse me, sir, I need help. I'm wondering if you can help me find this address." I turned around and there was Conrad!

I'm sure my shocked face must have been something to witness! Goosebumps erupted all over my body, and a feeling of indescribable yet visceral delight was coursing through me. It was simply beyond belief and rational explanation. It felt like the most amazing thing that had ever happened to me. Because we hadn't seen each other in years, Conrad was also rather surprised. I'm sure he was thinking, *What a lucky coincidence, running into an old friend!* He had no idea what I had set in motion through my request!

Conrad told me he and his wife didn't even live in Calgary anymore, and were only in my neighbourhood because a friend of his had called the day before, inviting them to see some new puppies. They had been driving around my neighbourhood trying to find the house, and I was the person they choose to ask for help. What were the chances? In a city of over one million people, the very person I asked for literally showed up at my doorstep only one day after asking the spirits we reconnect.

I was so overcome with joy and disbelief that I told Conrad the whole story. I remember him laughing and shaking his head. The great news was Conrad still had the program, was still willing to loan it to me, and was even able to deliver the CD the very next day, as he would just happen to be downtown for a meeting! To date, this is one of the most profound experiences of my life. I love telling this story to people and audiences around the world, as a way to clearly illustrate that the spirit world, our angels and guides, want to help us and want to be actively involved in our lives. We just need to ask and then let them do their work.

Sadly, most of us don't believe this is a two-way communication. We don't trust these conversations can be had. This story illustrates a real and potent ask for help, along with the expectation of being provided with an answer, actually works. Whether it's through somebody showing up on your doorstep, or having a blue jay feather or a dime cross your path, the spirit world hears you and delights in responding to your requests.

You are guided and loved every step of the way.

CHAPTER 7

Searching for My Spirit

By day, I was an employee at an office-furniture company, and by night a psychic medium. That was my life at the time. Although more and more people knew about my "other" work, I wasn't part of a community of like-minded souls. After a while it started to feel like something was missing.

One day, just flipping channels on the TV, I saw the world-renowned psychic Sylvia Browne. Watching another psychic in action was kind of a novel concept, and I was rather intrigued. I sought out her books and paid increasing attention when she was a guest on talk shows. The more I learned about her, the more I sensed she was authentic. I found out she had founded a church in California, called the Society of Novus Spiritus. It was based on gnostic principles, such as the duality of God as both masculine and feminine, a belief in reincarnation, and a conviction that humans are able to directly communicate with the divine and learn important things about their own soul's journey. There had been so much I disliked about traditional religion growing up, so these concepts were like a breath of fresh air and appealed to me right away. As I learned more about Gnosticism, I felt it resonating in a very deep place within. As my research continued I discovered there weren't any Canadian chapters of Novus Spiritus. Although there were a few study groups, none were in the Calgary area.

My wife had also become interested in the gnostic concepts, as well as Browne's church, and together we decided to form a study group. It gained popularity pretty quickly, especially among the people who came to me for readings. The idea to start our own Novus Spiritus Church in Calgary gained momentum, and we decided to approach Browne's organization and ask if they'd be open to a Canadian chapter. To our delight, they liked the idea! They also agreed to send their head minister to Calgary to run a Minister-In-Training program.

Prior to this, it had never occurred to me that I might even be remotely interested in becoming a minister. That was something just *not* on my radar. But the gnostic beliefs and principles were like a balm and a bright light, all at the same time. They soothed places in me I didn't even know needed healing, and they resonated in a very deep place within. I wanted to be able to help other people who had also suffered with the fire-and-brimstone philosophy of the church. I wanted them to know there was another, more open and compassionate, belief system. There was an alternative to mainstream religion.

To do so I first had to overcome a debilitating fear of public speaking. During the minister training we had to practice speaking to an audience, and the first time I did this was terrifying. I tried to be as prepared as I could, and had even written out a speech, but when I tried to deliver it I couldn't get the words out. I choked up and stuttered and thought I was going to have to leave the stage. But while I was standing there in front of so many people for the first time, I had a bit of an epiphany. I knew what I had to do was to simply speak from my heart. I took a really deep breath, put my notes aside, and just started talking about what I knew and about what I had experienced. At the end people actually got up and clapped, and it validated this approach; one I continue to use to this day. I speak my truth from my heart, and just trust. This was an important lesson for me to learn early in my career, especially considering the number of times over the ensuing years where I have needed to communicate my messages to large audiences—whether in person, online, on TV, or on the radio.

During the training program we were also exposed to the idea of past lives, as well as the ability we all have to learn more about them. This wasn't something I had ever given much thought, and if I had I would likely have been skeptical. Who knew that training to be a minister would involve a past-life regression while under hypnosis? But it did! And it's an experience which utterly changed the course of my life.

One of the Novus Spiritus people, named Ian Winston, came to Calgary to give our community more information about the concept of past lives. About thirty-five of us had gathered, and Ian, who was a certified hypnotist, presented his talk before offering to do a group regression for audience members. I was open to the idea, but had no idea if anything would happen. I was hopeful and nervous at the same time.

Using techniques to relax us, Ian asked us to let our logical minds rest and just trust whatever it was we saw or heard or experienced with no judgment. I remember him saying, "Just pay attention and observe and be aware." As soon as I did this I could see myself standing in a farmers field. I looked at my feet and could see I was wearing boots with brown pants, and a white, puffy shirt with the sleeves rolled up. I had white skin and dirty blonde hair that hung past my shoulders, tied in a ponytail. I also saw that I had a tool in my hand, and I knew I was using it for my work in the field. I had a feeling it was the 1200s, and that I was in Southern France. I also knew I was a Christian, but I wasn't Catholic. I didn't know how I knew any of these things.

I looked behind me and saw a castle upon a hill. To my right was a little, elongated building, and in the middle was a blacksmith's work area. A man was hammering on a piece of metal, and sparks were flying off. He had a dark moustache and curly salt-and-pepper hair. His large belly was covered by a leather apron, and there was a fire blazing behind him. As I watched he looked up at me and smiled. I didn't expect to recognize him, but I did! At that moment, which felt very surreal, I knew this blacksmith was my father. Not only my father in that life, but in this one as well. It was the same person, even though they looked completely different.

Suddenly, something else happened that caught my attention. On another hill, about half a kilometre away, a switchback road zigzagged down from the top. Something white caught my eye. It looked as though a white horse was running down the hill, and as it got closer I could see there was a woman astride the horse. She was dressed completely in white, and had long, flowing blond hair down to her hips. There was no saddle on her horse, and as she rode to a stop in front of me the very first thing I noticed was how clean she looked. It made me realize that I was quite dirty. I felt attracted to her, but at the same time afraid. I knew I mustn't look her in the eyes, as she seemed like somebody very important—like a princess. Even so, I didn't know who she was so I kept my eyes down and tried to busy myself with the tool in my hands, scraping at the ground. She began to laugh and galloped around me in a circle. I didn't know what to do, and felt very awkward. Was I supposed to say something? Was I allowed to interact with her? What did she want? And then she was gone, and I was suddenly aware of Ian Winston's voice saying it was time to come back to the room, and to the present time, and to feel ourselves in our bodies again.

I was amazed by what had happened, but also confused. My mind was full of questions, but the biggest was whether I had really just remembered a past life, or whether I had just made the whole thing up. I remember chuckling to myself and thinking I had a pretty vivid imagination. Marissa and I went home that night, and although I knew we were both thinking about what had happened neither of us talked about it right away. We didn't mention it until the next morning, when she shook me from sleep to say she couldn't stop thinking about her experience and to ask me about mine.

"Mine was odd," she said. "I think it was Southern France, around the 1200s, and I was a princess or something. I was riding a horse and there was a castle, and I rode up to this farmer boy in a field. I thought he was really cute, and I started laughing at him and teasing him. He had dirty blonde hair and was wearing a puffy, pirate-type shirt. When I looked at him I knew it was you! I recognized you even though you looked totally different."

Her story shook me right out of sleep, and I sat bolt upright in bed. I couldn't believe it! And neither could she, once I explained I had experienced the same thing in the reverse. My logical mind went right to being skeptical, and I felt certain Ian must have made some specific hypnotic suggestions that would explain why we had the same experience. So, I called Ian up to ask if he had instructed us to imagine a life in France in the 1200s—and if he had suggested farmers or castles or horses! Ian assured me none of his suggestions were specific at all. He simply had us relax, and instructed us to feel comfortable and open to whatever surfaced.

When I told him about what had happened he was reassuring, and said sometimes couples who had shared past lives would have a similar experience in a past-life regression. I still wasn't convinced. I told him I needed all the phone numbers of the people in class because I intended to call everyone!

I did just that, and not one person's experience was even close to the same as ours. I found this incredibly profound, which was not to say that my logical mind didn't continue to interfere. It did, and I still wasn't completely convinced, but I definitely knew I wanted to find out more and wanted to continue to explore the notion of having lived more than once.

At that time I had no idea where this interest in past lives would take me. So much was soon to be revealed!

CHAPTER 8

Travelling Back in Time

Time passed, but I found I couldn't shake the past-life experience. I returned to it over and over in my mind, and found myself increasingly curious. I needed to know whether what we had experienced was real, or a figment of our imaginations. The fact Marissa had experienced the same life in the regression gave the event further validity, and she, too, was interested in finding out more.

We did research on life in Southern France during the 1200s, and discovered there *was* a group of non-Catholic Christians who lived in that region. To my delight and amazement, they were Gnostics! If I truly had lived the life of that farmer boy this may explain the deep resonance I felt with the gnostic-based teachings of the Novus Spiritus Church.

The faith was called Catharism, and differed from Catholicism in quite a few ways. They didn't accept the hierarchy of priests or the notion of hell. Even more heretical, at the time, they believed in reincarnation and the equality of the sexes. For all this, the Cathars suffered a prolonged period of persecution by the Catholic Church.

I also learned, in the early 1200s, the Cathars mostly resided in and around Languedoc in Southern France—in the foothills of the Pyrenees Mountains—and many of their castles were still standing. My wife and I scanned photos online, but it was hard to feel any sense of familiarity via the Internet. We started to talk about the prospect of actually going to France, as we felt the need to experience the region first-hand and see what we felt when we actually stepped foot on the land. When we learned the literal meaning of Languedoc is "language of *yes*," it pushed us over the edge and we begin to make this dream of ours a reality.

You can't visit France without going to Paris, right? We decided to start the trip with four days in the City of Light. We saw the Eiffel Tower and the Louvre, and we sat in outdoor cafés and drank espresso. I liked the thought that anyone encountering us would think we were average tourists; only we knew the real reason for our overseas trip.

On day five we took the high-speed rail train from Paris to Languedoc. It's not called "high-speed" for nothing! France's rail network is the fastest in Europe, reaching speeds of up to three-hundred and twenty km/hour. I knew it was fast because I actually felt my ears pop as we travelled through tunnels. We arranged to pick up our rental car in Carcassonne, located in the Languedoc-Roussillon region, and then drive on to Espéraza, the heart of Cathar country.

Many of the famous Cathar sites, including the castles, were only a short drive away. With only nine days in the area, the question was which ones we should visit. The task ahead seemed overwhelming, but I had an inner certainty we would find what we were looking for—and when we did, we'd know it.

We checked into our quaint bed and breakfast overlooking the Aude River, and were delighted to find our hosts, a French couple, spoke excellent English. We told them the story of our shared past life, discovered through hypnotic regression, and asked if they had ever heard legends about a "lady in white", or a princess, who rode horseback. They hadn't, but the man was quite knowledgeable about the Cathars and was able to recommend some castles he thought we should visit.

On our large map of the area he circled five spots of interest, all of them castles that had been around in the early 1200s. He recommended Château de Quéribus, Peyrepertuse, Puivert, Montségur, and the large Cathar castle in Carcassonne, the city where we'd picked up the car. We made an itinerary for our remaining days in France, planning to visit at least one castle per day.

First on our list was Château de Quéribus, fifty-three kilometres away. For such a compact car, our little blue Peugeot had great bursts of power and got us there quickly. It was imperative to keep up with the speedy (and somewhat crazy) French drivers, so my aggressive driving abilities were tested on a daily basis!

The castle at Quéribus is an abandoned ruin sitting atop boulders, seven-hundred and twenty-eight metres above ground level. We drove the steep road up to the castle, paid our entrance fee, and started to explore. The castle itself hadn't been very large, maybe only three or four rooms. As we wandered, I tried to get a feeling for the place and ended up connecting to the spirit of a young French woman who I could see baking bread in an old stone oven. It was interesting to be able to tap into the time period, and I definitely felt a deep connection to the time and the people, but this particular spot didn't feel like the one we had both seen. The topography was off, and there weren't any large fields like the one I had seen myself working as the farmer boy.

Only fifteen minutes away was Peyrepertuse, an imposing castle built on a limestone cliff. It is strategically located within sight of Château de Quéribus, so the inhabitants could signal each other in times of trouble. This second castle is right on the border of France and Spain, and was built to resist invading Spanish forces but ended up being used to defend against the Catholic Church. After a steep and strenuous eight-hundred-metre hike we were rewarded with a fabulous view of the surrounding countryside, and proceeded to check out the tourist shop. We tried asking if legends concerning a woman in white could be found in the local historical records, but no one seemed to understand and we left feeling a little worn out and discouraged.

The next day we went back to Carcassonne. The massive, double-walled castle actually housed an entire town—called La Cité—inside of it. There is quite a history to this enormous Cathar relic: it's the place where the crusading army surrounded the castle and forced a surrender. Initiated by the Catholic Church to eliminate Catharism, the castle was ruled by Raymond Roger Trencavel, a lord in the region. He was not a Cathar, but was of the belief that Cathars and Catholics could live harmoniously together. There was even a Catholic Church in La Cité.

When I heard Trencavel's name it instantly felt familiar, like I'd known him before, but I wasn't connecting to anything in the castle itself. I felt very sorrowful about what happened in that place, but it didn't feel like where I had lived as the farmer boy. When we left Carcassonne that day I was starting to wonder if we were ever going to find our past home. With all the Cathar Castles in the region the quest began to feel a little bit like searching for a needle in a haystack. I remember driving back to our bed and breakfast that evening, and wondered as we passed other Cathar Castles if any of them contained the answer.

The next day dawned clear and hot. We felt refreshed from a good night's sleep, and fortified by a terrific French breakfast of coffee and croissants. There were only two castles left on our list: Puivert and Montségur. We decided to travel to Montségur first because of its pivotal place in the history of the Cathars, and then on our way back would take in Puivert.

The Château de Montségur is probably the best known of all the Cathar Castles. Its name literally means "safe hill," and for a time the 1,200-metre high castle, poised atop a rocky mountain, was just that for the scores of dispossessed Cathar families seeking shelter from the Catholic Crusaders.

In 1243, a siege began at Montségur and 10,000 Royal Catholic troops surrounding the castle. The Pope had ordered the Cathars convert to Catholicism, or be killed. A pyre was erected at the bottom of the mountain. Inside, however, the Cathars had immense stores of food and water, and were able to hold out for ten months. When their resources became depleted, in March of 1244, the Cathars announced they would surrender, but wanted a fifteen-day truce. This gave them time to celebrate the spring equinox one last time.

On March 16, 1244, the last Cathars exited Montségur. It is said the just over two hundred residents linked hands, sang, and marched down the mountain. Of the 200,000 Cathars of France, they were all that was left after the crusades. When they reached the bottom of the mountain, every single one walked straight into the burning fire.

I thought of this incredibly moving story as Montségur came into view; of the Cathars who had held out to the end, and who would rather die than renounce what they believed. These amazing people would have rather be burned alive than live a lie. I found their story so inspiring, and, more than that, I felt an intense connection to this land and to these people. We stopped at the bottom of the mountain, where the pyre would have been, and found a tombstone with an inscription that read: *The Cathars, martyrs of pure Christian love. 16 March 1244.* I picked some wildflowers and laid them on the grave before beginning our ascent up the mountain. It was incredibly steep, but when we reached the top we were rewarded with an unbelievable view that stretched almost to the sea, hundreds of kilometres away. There was a French tour going on inside, and because we couldn't understand Marissa and I wandered around on our own. We walked slowly, exploring both the inside and the outside, getting a real feel for the place. There was a sense of deep familiarity, and I was moved to tears numerous times that day.

Leaving Montségur, we headed back toward our inn, stopping at the last Cathar castle on our list. Puivert looked nothing like the others. First of all, it was built at the top of a small hill, not a mountaintop. Second, it had the same turrets and towers, but its shape was more a square than a rectangle. As we drove up to the parking area Puivert seemed the most familiar to me, yet something was still a little off.

At the front gate, where there was a drawbridge entrance to the castle, a dark-haired young man sat at a kiosk, selling books and post cards, and giving out pamphlets. We had been having such little success with communicating and finding out information I almost didn't bother asking this fellow any questions. However, something nudged me to talk to him, and we discovered he spoke very good English. I told him how we'd been searching everywhere for stories about a woman in white, possibly a princess, who lived during the time of the Cathars. As I began to list off the places we'd been, he interrupted.

"I know exactly who you're talking about," he said.

"You do?" I exclaimed. Marissa and I exchanged looks of excitement.

"Yeah, I work here in the summer, but I'm a student majoring in history. I love the history of the Cathars." My heart was pounding as he continued. "There is a legend about the Lady in White here at Puivert, from the thirteenth century. It is said she was a princess in Aragon, Spain, and she was known for riding bareback on a white horse. She is said to have had long blonde hair."

Breathless, we urged him on.

"The castle was best known for the travelling troubadours who would visit once a year and play music and recite poetry. The legend goes that one year all the farmers'' fields flooded, and the troubadours could not come. The Lady in White loved the troubadours, and was very distressed. She had a special rock where she prayed, and went there to ask that the waters recede so the musicians and poets could return. On the day the water disappeared the Lady in White did as well, and was never seen or heard from again. The legend goes on to say she had given her life, or thrown herself into the water, to save the land and ensure the troubadours could return."

I had gone from being discouraged, imagining we would have to return home without any answers, to absolute elation. This was feeling very right, but something still didn't make sense. If this was the right place, why did the castle look unfamiliar? I asked our young guide.

"Probably because it's been rebuilt many times!" he responded. "Come, I'll show you. The original castle is back here."

He led us around the backside of the castle, which was mostly in ruins. As I walked around I saw the original imprints of pictures carved into the stone walls. They depicted musicians and large gatherings of people, and looked familiar to me. We walked through all the old rooms, and then up the spiralling stone staircase which led to the tower at the back of the castle and into a turret.

I looked out onto the land below and across to the hill. The same zigzagging road cutting down it, and I knew we had found the right place. As if to underscore the point, as I looked down into the fields, the young man said, "Puivert was a farming community that helped supply food for Carcassonne and the lands of Raymond Roger Trencavel. He was the lord of this land."

Goosebumps broke out all over my body. That's why Trencavel's name had felt so familiar! I knew what I needed to do. I practically flew down the narrow spiral staircase in my haste to get out to the fields below. I needed to stand in the exact spot I had as a farmer boy. As if being pulled by a magnet, I walked quickly until stopping at what felt like the right place. From there I could see the castle on the hill, and to my right were the ruins of the blacksmith shop. Just as it had been in my regression.

I knew at that moment, with absolute certainty, the past life Marissa and I had experienced together had been very real. There was no doubt in my mind that I had lived here, and that I had once stood in this very spot.

Eight hundred years later, I had returned home.

CHAPTER 9

Ghosts at The Rouge

Returning from France to my actual home in Canada was bittersweet. It felt as though I was leaving an important, although newly discovered, part of myself behind. Luckily, I was still connected to the Novus Spiritus group in Calgary, and that helped maintain a feeling of continuity between my passions, my calling, and my real life. Choosing to hang out with people who believed in some of the same things as I did was both enlivening and interesting.

I'll never forget one of the evenings we spent together at a local restaurant called The Rouge; a place purported to be haunted. I'd seen a TV show about the restaurant, where current and previous employees were interviewed and shared their experiences of many unexplained ghostly encounters, including frying pans moving on their own atop the stove, doors swinging open and closed, and the sound of a child's laughter when the building was completely empty except for one employee. The Rouge was a large heritage home built in 1891 by a man named Alfred Ernest Cross. The residence was in the oldest neighbourhood in Calgary—an area called Inglewood—and had housed his family, including a daughter named Lizzie who had died of influenza at a young age. Cross himself was a businessman, cattleman, and later a politician. Most famously, he was one of Calgary's Big Four, who contributed a quarter share to the founding of the first Calgary Stampede in 1912.

The show intrigued me, and I wanted to experience The Rouge for myself. I suggested it to the Novus Spiritus group, and a few of us arranged to meet up and have supper. I was very curious as to what I might feel or see in a place that was rumoured to be haunted. My nighttime flying experiences as a child, through the astral world, had stayed with me, and I had come to believe the older woman I'd once seen—wearing a long, dark Victorian-style dress and floating over the telephone poles—may have been a ghost as many traditionally think of them. I wanted to know more about this in-between world, and so the chance to perhaps see another ghost, right in my own city of Calgary, piqued my interest.

There were six of us who met for supper, and we sat in what had been the living room of the old house. The chef, renowned for his exquisite French cuisine, did not disappoint. What *was* disappointing was the fact I didn't see or feel a single thing. When we told the waiter we were interested in the restaurant's ghost stories, he regaled us with tales of lights flickering, the electricity going out completely, and doors flying shut on their own. As I listened I realized I truly had been expecting for something to happen, but as our dinner plates were cleared I became resigned to just enjoying the dessert and the company for the remainder of the evening. And that's when I saw him: a large man with a thick moustache, dressed in a brown period suit, was walking toward me.

He was middle-aged, heavy-set, and very tall—around 6'1". He was also very, very pale. Otherwise, the man looked just like you and I, very much flesh and blood, but both his colouring and his dated suit gave me pause. He just didn't look as though he belonged. I watched him walk toward our table, looking around to see if any of my friends could also see him, but they were all engaged in conversation and no one seemed to notice this large man approaching. As he drew level with our table he looked me right in the eye, and I felt a strange shiver pass through me. The man then walked by on my left side and tried to move in behind my chair. The only problem was my chair was right against a wall, with a window on the wall behind. I pulled in my chair for him to pass, still thinking this was a living and breathing person. He simply seemed so real.

The man shuffled behind my seat, but I couldn't feel him pass by. The space was so tight I knew I should be able to feel him brushing against me, or pushing against my chair. I turned to the right and that's when I witnessed the thing that made me realize the man was really a ghost: he walked right through the wall, face-first, and disappeared completely.

"Oh my God." I exclaimed. "Did you guys see that?"

My friends looked up from their dessert and conversation, and one of them asked, "See what?"

"That man in the brown suit! He just walked right through the wall!" I had full on goosebumps now, and kept looking back and forth between the wall he had just passed through and the incredulous faces of my friends. I proceeded to tell them the whole story, and they were pretty bummed out they hadn't seen what I'd seen! The next time the waiter came by, I said, "Listen, I think I just saw your ghost."

"Was it a child?" he asked. "We're all pretty sure the ghost is a child, maybe Cross's daughter who died. She plays tricks on us, and even locked someone in the fridge downstairs one day."

"I didn't see any kids, but I just saw a six-foot man pass through the wall."

The waiter's jaw dropped. "What did he look like?"

I described the apparition's height, his girth, his moustache, and the period suit.

The waiter smiled and said, "I'll be right back." A few minutes later he returned holding a framed photograph. "Is this the man you saw?"

"That's him!" I shouted in disbelief, staring at the photo of the man I had seen walking through the dining room.

"This is Alfred Ernest Cross, the man who built the house," said the waiter, shaking his head in amazement. "I'm curious, where did you see him walk through the wall? Which spot?"

I pointed to my right. "Right there."

"That makes sense," said the waiter. "There used to be a door there, the door to the kitchen. When the owner renovated the house to turn it into a restaurant he moved the door to the kitchen over there," he pointed behind his shoulder, "but it used to be right there."

I think it's safe to say everyone had a memorable evening! Although I returned to The Rouge a few more times after that night, I never saw Alfred Ernest Cross again. This experience, however, fuelled an interest in the paranormal; something which ended up manifesting a year later, all the way across the country!

CHAPTER 10

Faith Leads Me Home

Sometime after Marissa and I had returned from France we begin to notice the fabric of our Calgary neighbourhood shifting and changing, and not for the better. There was a real rise in crime and gang activity, which began to be felt in the area where we lived, and made me feel less and less comfortable in this ever-expanding Alberta city. I'll never forget the morning I woke to the sound of gunshots. When I looked out the window I actually saw people fleeing! In another instance a loaded gun was found in a nearby playground, where my kids regularly spent time. The last straw came when I witnessed a hold-up at a local Donair shop where I was having lunch.

With gun violence in my own neighbourhood, it felt as though it were on a rapid descent into unsafe territory. I was constantly looking over my shoulder, and I was afraid to let my kids walk anywhere on their own. I had never imagined our way of life would change so rapidly, and as it did I found myself longing for more safety and security. I thought often of how safe Nova Scotia had felt when I was growing up, and began to wonder if it might be possible for me to move my family back. I wanted my kids to finish growing up in a place where they could just go out and play and I wouldn't have to worry about their safety.

There were no transfer opportunities within the company I worked, and although I was making money from my readings it certainly wasn't enough to support a family. I realized that in order to return to the Maritimes I would need a new career. One day, while I was heading home from work and feeling the weight of responsibility, I decided I needed help. I remembered how quickly and decisively the universe had assisted me when I needed help finding Conrad, and I decided to put it to work on this situation. *Please help me figure out a way to get home to Nova Scotia*, I implored. At that exact moment a Canada Post truck drove by, and a light bulb went off.

Working for Canada Post would be perfect: it aligned with my need to be active, it was a government job that paid well, and, being a national organization, there might be a chance for a transfer to Nova Scotia. Plus, the fact my great-great-grandfather had been one of the first postmasters in Canada felt like a great sign. Why hadn't I thought of working for Canada Post before?! Still, I knew the universe had provided the perfect sign at just the right moment, so I quickly put the wheels in motion. I applied for a temporary position with Canada Post and immediately got three days of work. I knew this was another sign there was more to come, so I quit my job I had worked at for fifteen years and simply trusted the permanent position was on its way.

Within a week, three different mail carrier positions came up. I applied online, and was asked to come in for an aptitude test. My elation turned to massive disappointment when I walked in for the test and discovered I was one of two hundred applicants. Not only that, I discovered there were three other days of testing with a few more hundred people. But I told myself to have faith and not let this get me down. I wrote the test to the best of my abilities, and I did it fast. In fact, I was one of the first people done.

And then I waited. I had about two or three months salary saved up, but as the days turned into weeks and I still hadn't heard anything I started to panic. One day, I decided to take matters into my own hands. I got dressed as though I was going for an interview, and I showed up at the Calgary headquarters for Canada Post. It was a secure building, with a gate and a security guard sitting in a little shack out front. I walked up to the guard and announced myself, and said I had an appointment with the head of the HR department.

"Um, you're not in the book," he said, studying the schedule and scratching his head.

"Well, I should be in there. I have an appointment." I made a point of looking at my watch.

"How do you spell your name again?" The guard ran his finger down the page, mumbling. "I'm not supposed to let you in if you're not in the book."

I spelled out my last name and added, "Listen, my interview is in five minutes." I looked at my watch again. "I can't miss it; I really need this job."

The guard sighed and picked up the phone. "I'll call them," he said, causing my heart to pound while he dialled. He held the receiver to his ear for what seemed an eternity. "They're not answering." He placed the receiver back in its cradle. "They must have forgot to tell me."

He looked me over, as though to size up my danger level. I held my breath. "Here's your visitor's pass," he said reluctantly. "Go in these doors and all the way down the hall. HR is on the right."

I was grinning from ear to ear as I walked into the building, but, again, my excitement quickly transformed to dismay when I got to the HR department and saw it was a construction zone. No wonder they weren't answering the phone! Plastic tarps barricaded everything but a little bench off to the side. I sat down with a sigh, not understanding what the universe was up to. I'd actually gained access to the building, as well as the department I needed, but on a day when it was closed for renovations and there wasn't a soul around!

I sat there for a few minutes, wondering what to do next, when a woman came walking past. She did a double take and stopped. "Can I help you?"

"I'm here to meet with the head of HR." Having done my research, I dropped the name of the woman who I knew was in charge.

"Do you have an appointment?"

"No, but I'd really like to talk to her."

"Well, she's not even in the office today. I'm sorry."

It was then I made a decision that changed my life: I told this woman my whole story. I told her about the gun violence in our neighbourhood, and how I really wanted to figure out a way to get back to Nova Scotia for my kids. I told her I had quit my job, and we were running out of money, and I really wanted to work for Canada Post. I told her I had taken the aptitude test, but had not heard any news. I even told her about my great-great-grandfather! And I wrapped it all up by saying I was running on blind faith, but I felt strongly I was supposed to be a mail carrier.

To my delight, that's when she told me she actually worked for the HR department, and just that morning another position had opened. "I was going to go through the aptitude tests today to see who was next on the list, but you're right here! Why don't I look and see how you did. What's your name?"

I told her and she walked off beyond the plastic wall. I was pretty sure I'd done well on the test, but I tried not to get my hopes up. She came back with a file in hand. "Well, you didn't do the best, but you weren't the worst either. In fact, you did pretty well; you're in the seventy-five percentile."

She paused, looked up at me, and smiled. "Can you start on Monday?"

Thus was the magical beginning of my Canada Post adventure. I started as a temporary employee, filling in for people who were off on holiday or had called in sick, but within a year had moved into a full-time position. I even got lucky with a great job in my own neighbourhood, making deliveries by truck to community mailboxes and businesses.

On the day I was notified of my full-time, permanent status, I applied for a transfer. I knew it could still be a while before I was transferred, but I gave them three locations in Nova Scotia to broaden my chances. In the meantime I worked my butt off: delivering mail by day, doing readings by night, and hoping we all stayed safe until it was time to move.

It took eighteen months, but the day finally came; I got the phone call I'd been waiting for. My transfer had been granted, and I would be delivering mail in Halifax. I had two weeks to get there and claim my spot, so I packed our PT Cruiser with some personal items and set off across the country. I was determined to find a home for my family and make a new start in the place I had first called home.

CHAPTER 11

Paper Messages by Day, Spirit by Night

The first order of business was finding a place to live. I'd got used to the exorbitant housing prices in Calgary, and was pleasantly surprised to remember that a house in rural Nova Scotia, with a little bit of land, didn't have to cost a million dollars!

I found a place in Hammonds Plains; a small community within easy commuting distance to Halifax, and that had lots of space for our kids to play outside. After living in a huge city with a million-plus people, a place where I had come to fear for my children's safety, being back home felt comforting and secure. Marissa and the kids soon joined me, and we all settled in.

Word of mouth followed me back to Nova Scotia, and I began to again book evening readings. Although we were in a new place, my life as I knew it resumed: I delivered paper messages by day, and spirit messages by night. I'd even built a little office beside the house to keep the business separate from home. I thought it would help my wife with some of her increasing worries about my work as a medium. Before we left Calgary I'd done some work for the police, and it had become public. Marissa was very uncomfortable with the possibility some of the criminals I'd brought to justice might know my name, and so be able to find our family.

In order to build up the same solid client base I'd had in Calgary, I knew I would need to get out and start meeting people. My ultimate goal was to one day be able to leave Canada Post and work solely as a medium. Yet in order to do that I needed to become known for my abilities in Nova Scotia. After all, although I'd grown-up in the province, I'd never worked here as a medium!

I discovered a local spiritualist church where people were conducting readings. I went to check them out, and despite not being blown away by what I witnessed I could see the people receiving the messages were being helped and enlightened in some way. I knew this was the next step for my career. I'd been doing individual readings for many years, and through my minister training I'd gained some valuable experience talking to groups. Although standing up in front of people still made me nervous, I knew this was an important part of my path. I offered the group my services as a medium, telling of my background in the Novus Spiritus tradition. I needed to see if the work of connecting with spirit and allowing their messages to come through could be done while standing in front of a group.

My first experience went really well, despite being quite nervous. It was a small group of around thirty people, and as

I had already got to know a few of them it didn't feel as though I were facing a room full of strangers. I first gave a talk about my experiences connecting with spirit, and then it was time to see who came through. This involves literally flipping a switch in my mind, where I go from speaking to a form of deep listening. It's necessary for my awareness to shift from the external world to my own internal world, where I can see, feel, hear, and allow those internal senses to guide. Only then can I give the messages to those waiting. Up until that moment I hadn't any experience doing this in front of a group, but what I found was the process was the same.

I tuned in and immediately began to see drumsticks. I felt this message was coming from a father who had passed and was meant for his son, who was in the room. I voiced this and a young man spoke up.

"I'm a drummer, and I design mallets for drums."

Bingo. "Okay, this is for you then. Your father is coming through. I feel like he hasn't passed all that long ago. He's showing me a place where you used to walk together. Looks like Point Pleasant Park?"

The man nodded slowly, tears in his eyes.

"He wants you to know he still walks there with you."

The young man went on to explain that he and his father would take walks at the park during the last year of his life. The son still walked there, and often thought of his dad.

"When you're thinking of him like that, he's right there with you. You're not just remembering. He's there and he wants you to know that."

The spiritualist church asked me to come back again and I did, to increasing numbers of people each week. Doing these small readings was a great way to build my confidence, but something was going on behind the scenes of which I wasn't aware. Apparently, few of the other mediums in the church had begun to spread rumours about me that weren't true, but which elicited the attention of the head minister, a woman from Montreal. She came to investigate, and ended up firing the other mediums for spreading lies.

The experience helped me learn a valuable lesson, similar to the one I'd learned through Novus Spiritus. Simply put, being involved in any organization where people's egos got in the way and they feel a need to compete just isn't my scene. I realized with, crystal-like clarity, that I didn't need to be part of a group or a team or a religion. I just had to be me—my own person—and focus on the work I felt a deep call to do. This work was about helping people to heal their lives and move beyond grief; helping them to see their loved ones are still with them, just in a different form, and are fully able to communicate.

That was the end of my membership in organizations, although my involvement in both Novus Spiritus and the spiritualist church helped me grow as both a medium and a person.

CHAPTER 12

Thy Will Be Done

One benefit of being back in Nova Scotia was again being close to my mom. She had missed all of us, especially her grandkids, and we made a point of spending a lot of time together. My mom remarried the year I moved to Calgary, and her new husband, Larry, was a great guy. I still really missed having my dad around, but I also wanted my mom to be happy and couldn't have wished for a better match.

Larry, a former air force captain, was hardworking, loyal, kind, and helpful. I was excited moving back home allowed me and my family to spend more time with both of them. Larry was also analytical and methodical—a measure twice, cut once kind of guy—and so had doubts about my work as a medium. One day his mom came through to me loud and clear. I got her first name, which I hadn't known.

"How the hell would you know that?" he asked.

"This is what I do, Larry." I laughed.

Every so often I would surprise him with a little piece of information there was no way I could have known. Like the time his mom told me about how she used to make Larry his favourite pudding. So, what I did I do? I presented Larry with some sticky toffee pudding the next time he was over. "This is just like my mom's." His face softened and he looked quizzically at me.

"I know, Larry," I said simply.

Being handy with tools, Larry loved to help out. One day, after we'd moved into the house in Hammonds Plains, he came over to help hang my clothesline. While there he complained about a headache. I gave him some Tylenol and didn't think anything of it, but later in the day a strange thing happened. He left the garage to go into the house for something, and as he did I could see a dark mass at the base of his skull. It was there for only a moment and then gone, yet the image stayed with me the rest of the day. I couldn't shake it. I didn't want to believe what I'd seen. *Why would I see that?* I asked myself. *I've got to be wrong.*

Then the following weekend at my daughter's Highland dance recital, where I had expected to see Larry, my mom said he couldn't come because he still had that damn headache. "I'm worried about him," my mom whispered. "He's never had a headache for a full week before. And no amount of pills make the pain go away."

I knew then what I'd seen had likely been true: the dark mass had looked like a brain tumour. "Mom, I need you to go home right now. I want you to take Larry to the hospital."

She gasped, a look of alarm now on her face. "What?"

I knew I had to tell her everything. "I don't want to scare or worry you, but last week I saw something in the back of his head while he was helping with the clothesline. I wanted it to be nothing, so I didn't tell anyone. I still hope I'm wrong, but I think you should get him checked out right away."

My mom scurried out of there, and hastened to the hospital. The doctors did a scan and found a mass on the back of Larry's brain stem. Two days later he had surgery to see if it was cancerous. The test came back positive, but the results also showed the cancer hadn't originated in the brain. With a full body scan we found the cancer was in most of Larry's organs; it was all the way up his spine. The brain was the last place it took hold—and the point of recovery was long past.

I was so mad when I heard the news. Mad at myself; because I'm supposed to see these kinds of things and be able to help the people I love. I was also angry and disappointed in the spirit world. By the time I saw the cancer it had been too late. Why show me now? Why not tell me with enough time?

Larry went downhill quickly and I spent a lot of time at their house, trying to make up for lost time. I wanted to connect with this man in order to better understand his journey, and to perhaps help him in some way. He was never religious, and certainly skeptical about what I did, but in those last couple of months Larry was open and curious. And I was more than happy to tell him what I knew to be true.

"When it's your time, when you're passing over, Larry, you're going to see a beautiful white light."

"That's just an old wives tale. When it's over its lights out!" He chuckled. "Aren't we just done?"

"I've seen it myself, Larry. I can guarantee it will be the most incredible thing you've ever seen."

He was silent, but didn't take his eyes off me.

I continued. "When you see it, I want you to go toward the light. That's our true home, and from where we all come." I paused, and I could see tears glinting in his eyes.

"Do you really think I'll see a light, Shawn?"

"I don't just think it; I *know* it."

My certainty seemed to reassure him, and I felt happy I could play a role in the final days of this good man's life. What I most wanted was to somehow facilitate a healing, so Larry and my mom could have a few more years together; a few more trips to their cabin in Newfoundland, a few more fishing expeditions. We tried praying with good intentions, positive thinking, and hands-on healing, but despite it all, and within only two months of the surgery, Larry died. The only consolation was he appeared not to have suffered too much.

I was at the house the night before he passed. As Larry didn't want to die in the house, he and my mom had made a pact to go to the hospital, which was in Truro, the nearest town. He told my mom he would let her know when it was time, and that's exactly what he did. Up until then, Larry had spent most of his time sleeping, but on this particular night he suddenly woke and yelled out, "Truro!" Then he collapsed.

The ambulance came quickly, but because of the size of our doorframes the stretcher couldn't be brought in the house. I picked Larry up and carried him to the ambulance. He weighed about seventy-five pounds. As I lay him on the stretcher I reminded him about the light. I also made a special request.

"Larry, I know you can hear me. And I want you to do something for me. I want you to send me a sign. So I know you found the light and you made it home, okay? Send me a sign?"

I didn't have to wait long. The next morning my mom called from the hospital to say Larry had passed. We all got in the car—my wife, my kids, and Patsy (an aunt who had been staying with us). On the way to the hospital I told Patsy I'd asked Larry for a sign, and I knew we were going to get one. A few minutes later, I spotted an eagle in the sky.

"You see that, Patsy?"

"Yeah, I see that. It's just an eagle."

Even though the eagle was high above, I was certain this was Larry's sign. Which is why I was the only one not completely surprised when the eagle suddenly dropped from the sky and dive-bombed our car.

I was driving one hundred kilometres per hour, and this eagle not only aimed itself right at our vehicle but as it came closer it turned sideways and swept across the whole front of the windshield. Its wings were fully spread, the tip of one lightly touching the pavement. I had to jam on the brakes or I would have hit and killed the magnificent creature.

"Do you think it's just an eagle now?" I asked, watching as it soared back into the sky, my heart thumping in my chest.

Aunt Patsy burst into tears. "Oh my God, you weren't shitting me." She cried. "That's the most spiritual experience I've ever had in my whole life."

I said a silent thank you to Larry, and had a private chuckle over his intensity. He sure didn't want me to miss his message.

A few days later I spoke at Larry's funeral and said the Lord's Prayer, but it wasn't until later, back at home, did I finally understand why things happened with Larry the way they did. I had been so angry I hadn't been able to save him, but one line of that prayer kept nagging: *Thy will be done.*

The Lord's Prayer had never meant anything to me until that moment. But that day, that one line suddenly made a whole lot of sense. No matter how much we prayed over Larry or tried to heal his cancer, it wouldn't have done any good. I now thought maybe it was because a higher will we couldn't understand had prevailed.

This lesson has stayed with me. Through Larry's death I learned everyone has a time, and when it's your time to go that's it; nobody can change it. There's a bigger will going on, one that has nothing to do with what I might want for someone else. Not being able to see Larry's cancer earlier, and not being able to heal him, showed me I had a different role to play than the one I had supposed. Helping Larry make his transition was a huge honour, and one that has expanded my experience of love.

CHAPTER 13

Spirit Communication

After Larry's funeral the dust settled somewhat. Our family continued to adjust to life in a new province, but it was becoming more and more obvious my wife and I weren't happy in our relationship. She wanted me to revert to the man I had been when we were first married—someone who wasn't a psychic medium—and I knew I couldn't. In fact, I spent an increasing amount of time thinking about how I could quit my job and transition to doing this work I loved full-time. I truly believed I was helping to heal hearts, and the idea of spending whole days doing this beautiful and meaningful work felt as though I was fulfilling my soul's true purpose.

Unfortunately, fear got in the way. Fear told me I should stay in my relationship and stay with my work as a mail carrier. I was afraid of what divorce would mean for our kids, and I was afraid of not having enough money. In those days, fear was keeping me small and not allowing me to become who I was meant to be.

It was during this time I had a few physical encounters with the spirit world which solidified the notion that working with spirit really was my life's calling. These experiences also changed what I had known, up to that point, about how spirit can appear and connect.

I was delivering mail in the Hydrostone area of Halifax, and walked up the steps of an office building. I hadn't seen anyone at the top, but when I got there a man was holding the door open. He looked just like my Great Uncle Rob, but maybe forty years younger. A good-looking, vibrant, healthy, and happy man—smiling at me from ear to ear. I was quite struck by the resemblance to my great uncle, and also by the presence of this man. He seemed to be standing there just for me, smiling and attentive. I thanked him and walked through the door, and as I did my phone rang.

"Did you hear the news?" It was my mother.

"No, what news?"

"Your Great Uncle Rob passed."

Oh my God. It *was* him. I ran to the door and flew back down the stairs, scanning up and down the street. He was gone. Completely vanished.

"Shawn? Are you there?"

"Yeah, yeah. I'm here." I stood on the street, shaking my head and marvelling at it all.

"Mom, you're not going to believe this, but I'm pretty sure I just saw Uncle Rob."

"What?!"

"He just held the door open for me at a building on Kaye Street. It was him, letting me know he's okay; that he's better than okay, actually."

It wasn't until I hung up that I remembered the last time I

saw my Great Uncle Rob had been at Larry's funeral. He was in a wheelchair, and was hooked up to an oxygen machine. Rob was my mom's uncle and had been a heavy smoker his whole life. He'd been diagnosed with lung cancer and the prognosis wasn't good. Although in his late seventies he looked older when I saw him; a small and shrivelled version of who he had been.

"Rob, you shouldn't be here," I had said, bending low over the wheelchair and taking his hand.

"I couldn't miss saying goodbye to Larry," he whispered hoarsely. "My time's coming soon, Shawn. I have to be okay with this."

I squeezed his hand. "I probably won't get to see you again, but I want to ask you something. When you go, can you please visit me?"

"I will." His eyes glistened with tears.

It was my turn to choke back my emotions. "And when you get there, please tell Larry I said hi and I love him."

We parted ways after one last hug, and one last look into each other's eyes. Now here I was, standing on the street on a sunny day in Halifax, phone in hand, in awe at what had happened. He'd done it; my Uncle Rob was good to his word. And he hadn't found just any old way to communicate with me—he hadn't sent a feather or an eagle or a song on the radio—he'd sent himself! A version many decades younger, looking strong and cheerful and happy. He had paid me a most extraordinary visit, on the very day he passed from this earth, clearly showing me how well he now was.

This experience left me reeling, and also fascinated and newly curious about all the ways spirit can communicate with us. It occurred to me, in those days after seeing the flesh and blood version of Uncle Rob, that there is really no limit to how spirit communicates and shows up for us. It's only our own beliefs about what is possible and not possible that stop them sometimes from appearing.

Seeing Uncle Rob was the first time since becoming a medium that a spirit had visited in the human form. It got me thinking about my early childhood and my spirit guide Sam, and about how real he had been despite the fact no one else could see him. I also recalled how my great-grandparents were once present in physical form in my childhood bed during the night, how this "realness" had scared me. I remembered how I had basically vanquished them from my life by asking them to leave. It took the visit from Rob to feel a bit sad and regretful about that.

I then started thinking about how nice it would be to see my great-grandparents again, and the experience with Rob made me realize this was possible. A few weeks later, walking down another street in Halifax delivering mail, an older gentleman appeared in front of me from out of nowhere. I had been starting up a walkway when suddenly, on this quiet street, was a man who looked an awful lot like my great-grandfather.

"I'll take that for you," he said.

I must have looked at him curiously because he repeated himself. "I'll put that in the mail box for you."

My gut was telling me I was having another "Uncle Rob" moment; there was something quite surreal about this encounter. Still, my logical brain questioned it. *This guy must just live here,* I thought, giving my head a shake. I handed him the mail and turned to leave. The only thing was, as I walked away, I didn't hear the door and I didn't hear the mail slot. I turned around. He was gone. It was exactly the same thing that happened with Uncle Rob. This older man had completely disappeared, in the space of about three seconds.

If you take anything from this chapter I would like it to be this: trust yourself. We all have ideas of what spirit connection and communication looks like, sometimes largely based on books or movies concerning ghosts, but they're not all wispy beings who walk through walls. I can tell you with certainty that some are as physical as you and I. There's a Bible verse from the Old Testament I think is especially apt here. "Do not be forgetful to entertain strangers for thereby some have entertained angels unawares" (KJV, Hebrews 13.2).

If you think back over your life, you'll probably remember certain encounters with strangers that have been meaningful in some way. Perhaps someone said something which altered a course of thinking for the better. Maybe you were delayed while in a hurry, only to realize later the delay saved you from a car accident. We simply cannot know how often spirit is communing with us, or in what ways, but I'd like to encourage you to be open to how you are being guided and supported.

I know, without a doubt, we all have people watching over us, so the next time you have an odd encounter on the street or in the grocery store—something which feels a little bit surreal or supernatural—do yourself a favour and turn around when the other person walks away. They may have just vanished into the light! And then you'll know.

CHAPTER 14

Leaving and Finding

While my wife and I definitely had a strong past-life connection, it became clear to both of us we weren't meant to be married to each other for our whole lives. We decided to separate, and soon after divorced. I truly believe Marissa and I were meant to learn from each other in this life, and I'm grateful for all the experiences and all the love we shared—even the hard times.

After our separation there were, of course, many logistics to work out. I needed to find another place to live, and we needed to come up with a schedule that worked for the kids. Once everything was finally in place I began to feel a renewed sense of movement and possibility in my life. I felt free to make decisions I felt were good for me. The biggest way this manifested was being able to start putting more energy into the work I really loved. This meant I began to follow both my heart and my intuition when it came to my work as a psychic medium.

I felt strongly the urge to start doing live shows, even though I had a good amount of fear at the thought. What if I couldn't read people in a large group? What if I got up there and nothing happened? I had already proven to myself I could do readings in small group gatherings, like the ones at the local spiritualist church. There I had received valuable, clear information and validation the spirit was ready to communicate, even in a group setting. I had long been drawn to trying this out with a much larger group, and in the wake of suddenly being on my own I saw no reason not to try.

I brought in a guy I'd grown-up with, Darrell, to help with the organization. Word of mouth was spreading about who I was and what I did, and we ended up selling eighty-five tickets. I was really happy about the amount of people, and although I was nervous the whole event went really well. The connections with spirit were solid, and afterwards I heard positive reports from a number of people. I even got some good press and social media exposure.

The success of this first show seemed like a sign from the Great Spirit that I didn't need to worry about clinging to the security of my Canada Post job. Freed from some of the fears which had been my constant over the last few years I began to trust in my gift more, and believed in the guidance I received. In fact, it was during this time I became acquainted with a guide I didn't know I had—one who would help me face more of my fears and begin to walk more fully into my destiny.

She came to me in a dream. I appeared to be in Scotland, and in the dream a beautiful barefoot woman, wearing an intricately designed white gown, descended a hill by a river and came toward me.

She wasn't very tall, probably about five foot two or three, but had dark hair and stunningly beautiful, light-filled eyes. I felt a loving, confident, strong, and determined energy emitting from her. Her presence instantly made me feel safe.

"Shawn, I am Victoria," she said, a Gaelic lilt to her voice. "I want you to know I'm going to be helping you from now on with the work you're doing." I knew she wasn't talking about my job as a letter carrier!

"Are you a new guide?" I asked her.

"I've always been here, but I've not been working much with you. You need me now more than ever, so I will become more present." She went on to explain she would be my guide for all the work I was doing, connecting to spirits and different levels of energy. Victoria promised to protect me during this journey, and when she said that I felt very, very safe.

"Well, thank you. It's nice to meet you," I said. I then promptly woke up, the Scotland scene vanishing from sight, but I was left with a feeling of excitement at this new connection.

This amazing encounter felt so very real, and I didn't doubt for a second Victoria was at my side. I began to have an inner dialogue with her, and strongly felt her directing me to seek out spiritual wisdom via books and spiritual writers. I believe Victoria led me to authors like Wayne Dyer, Anita Moorjani, and Eckhart Tolle. Expanding my wisdom base gave me a new vocabulary which enabled me to help people in deeper ways, giving them a kind of tangible and practical guidance. Finding out about a new guide also made me more eager than ever to bring my childhood friend, Sam, back into my conscious awareness. It didn't take much for him to make his presence known.

I began doing daily spirit guide meditations with the intent and purpose to connect with Sam. These guided meditations were pretty relaxing, so I sometimes fell asleep. I remember telling Sam that if I fell asleep I wanted him to wake me up, but I was still not expecting for someone, just as I was drifting off, to grab my arm, pick it up, and drop it on the bed. That was amazing enough, but what came next really blew me away. It was as though I were watching a stone being dropped into a pond, and witnessing the subsequent ripples fanning out. Intense, tingling energy spread from my arm and all the way through my body. I had never felt anything like it. It was like light poured through me, touching every cell and every fibre of my being. In that moment I saw Sam's face and he smiled at me, light sparkling through both of us. I knew he had been there all along, and whenever I needed him in the future I knew he would still be right there.

I want you to know all of us have guides, and all of us have the ability to connect with them. If you're interested in finding out more about your guides (including their names), talk to them and ask they communicate. Practice meditation with the intention of connecting to your guide, and tell them you'd like the chance to hear them, see them, and experience them. Tell them you'll be open and receptive to any form of communication, including dreams, thoughts, or messages you hear out in the world. For example, you may begin noticing the same name repeated over and over in different circles. (This may be your guide's way of saying, "Hey, that's me!") Sam and Victoria are very special, and hugely important in my life. I feel their support and guidance every day. I know with absolute certainty none of us are ever alone, and it's a great gift when we all realize this. Please take advantage of the free guided meditation on my website, as it may help you make a connection to your own spirit guides. Once you experience the kind of love our spirit guides have for us, you'll never feel alone again. That's my hope and wish for you.

Having two spirit guides who are very different is rather interesting. Sam provides me with a gentle, easygoing, and fun energy, while Victoria really means business. (As you'll see in the next chapter, when she said she was going to protect me, she meant it.)

CHAPTER 15

Paranormal and Pirates

I was having more and more experiences that served to expand my understanding of what form spirit can take, and how spirit communicates. I felt hungry to explore this area further, so when I was invited to join a paranormal group in Halifax I leapt at the chance.

I had my own ideas about what was happening with these random spirits I could connect to—namely that they were having trouble finding and moving into the light. This, I believe, is the one place we are all meant to go. For whatever reason, however, some spirits do not allow themselves to transition. I call this in-between place they inhabit the astral world. This is where I believe some people get lost, or stuck. Perhaps due to fear, or some kind of worry there really is no afterlife.

From what I've witnessed, those who stuck on the earth

plane are very much still in their egos, and usually inhabit the same place they lived (or died).

Such was the case with the spirit of the pirate we encountered during one of my very first outings with the paranormal group. We went to Point Pleasant Park at nighttime with a film crew, and sat at a picnic table near the Prince of Wales Tower. As I was about to address the group I heard my spirit guide, Victoria, clearly say, "They will be no good." I knew she was warning me the spirits we would connect to at the park were low-level energies who had not yet moved into the light. I heard her warning and felt thankful for her presence, but I was still intrigued to find out more about who was there. As the leader of the group I led us in a spirit circle, where everyone held hands; left hand facing up, right hand facing down. This is a way to intentionally and communally connect our energy and help bridge the gap between this world and the other.

After Victoria sounded her warning, which had come as a mere whisper, she began talking in such a loud voice I initially believed one of the other women at the table was speaking. After a few minutes of confusion, I realized it was Victoria. She was repeating a single word I wasn't familiar with, and didn't understand. It sounded like "kidge" or "kedge". Although no one else in the circle could hear her, Victoria's voice was easily recorded on the devices we brought. (See note at the end of this chapter.)

It didn't take long to feel someone else around us, and the feeling wasn't very friendly or welcoming. This sense was soon confirmed when I asked aloud if the spirit was connected to this place. I heard the most blood-curdling growl, as if the spirit had bent low right over my ear. It sounded like the devil himself! I nearly jumped off the picnic table, and was surprised to hear the cameraman sitting beside me say, "What the hell was that?"

Later we talked and he admitted to also having heard the growl; he was so terrified he nearly dropped the camera and ran! I, too, was certainly frightened, but with Victoria on my team I knew I was protected—a power she was soon to show first-hand.

"Who are you?" I asked. "Are you somehow connected to this place?"

No further growls met my question, but I could definitely feel the energy of this spirit. I began to have a mental image, and he looked very much like what one may think of as a pirate. The name Edward suddenly came through. At the same moment the woman across from me yelled, "Somebody just grabbed me!"

Over the course of the next thirty minutes nearly everyone at the table felt they were either grabbed or pushed by the spirit, myself included. I could actually feel his fingers digging into my arm. I knew he was trying to scare us, and wanted us to leave.

I repeated myself. "Are you from this place? Are you connected to this building?" Again I heard my guide say the same words as before: "Go to the kedge".

At this point the cameraman had his camera trained on me because I was the one attempting to communicate with the spirit. So, what happened next was actually caught on film: the spirit put his hand on my back and pushed. When looking at the footage you can see his handprint on the back of my jacket, and you can see how I am propelled forward by this invisible hand.

Also on the tape is the voice of Victoria, saying sternly, "Get off Shawn." And he did. At that point, and on Victoria's urging, I asked God and the Great Spirit to surround us all with white light. Instantly I felt the energy of the place change, and could feel a collective and relieved sigh around the table. I could no longer feel the energy of the pirate's spirit. Later, I wondered if our gathering there, and bringing the light, finally helped him transition and move on.

That night in Point Pleasant Park remains the most vivid paranormal experience I've ever had, and bolstered by what I discovered I did a little research after the fact. Turns out, there was a man by the name of Edward Jordan (1771–1809), who was born in Ireland and took part in the Irish rebellions of 1797-98. He was sentenced to death, but turned informant and was pardoned. Jordan attempted to start a new life in Nova Scotia as a fisherman, with the help of a creditor. Even so, he had mounting debt and sought help from the merchants J&J Tremaine, who, after initially funding him, realized he was not going to be able to pay. The merchants sent Captain John Stairs to seize Jordan's fishing schooner, which was in the Gaspé. Stairs offered Jordan and his wife safe passage back to Halifax, but on the trip back in September of 1809 Jordan tried to take his ship back and slaughtered the crew. Unbeknownst to Jordan, the captain survived and was rescued by a passing fishing schooner. Stairs told the authorities, and Jordan was tried. Found guilty, he was hung at Black Rock Beach in Point Pleasant Park. His body was tarred and feathered, and hung in a gibbet as a warning to other pirates. His skull still resides at the Maritime Museum of the Atlantic in Halifax.

I discovered the place where people were hung was where the park's giant iron anchor lay now. I also found out "kedge" is the Gaelic word for anchor. When she used that word Victoria was trying to give me a landmark for where the spirit had lost his life.

I do believe our spirits maintain an energetic connection to where we die, so it makes sense this man may still have been hanging around the park. I've been back numerous times since that night, but I've never run into him again. I'd like to think we actually did help him move on into the light.

I've had other experiences with spirits who seem stuck and in need of some assistance moving out of their low-level energy place and into the light. Over time, what has become evident is there are also beings—you can call them guides or angels—who are already in the light but are there to help. I encountered one such being on McNabs Island after my Point Pleasant Park experience.

It was yet another outing with the paranormal group, and we decided to check out McNabs Island, a place in Halifax Harbour with a rich history. The island has numerous forts from various time periods, and so we explored one of the older ruins. We found tunnels leading underground, and as we descended I was instantly aware of the spirit of a man. He didn't seem frightening in the same way as Edward Jordan. Rather, this spirit appeared seemed more lost and confused. I was attempting to connect with him and encourage him to move toward the light when an amazing thing happened.

A ball of light, also known as an orb (which was actually visible later on film), came down through the ceiling. I felt somebody else enter the room. This spirit stood behind me and spoke Mi'kmaq. At one point I actually felt his hand on my back, pushing me hard enough I stumbled forward. At the same time, there was a strong and overpowering smell of smoke. I recognized it as burning sweetgrass and sage, although there was no visible smoke. It wasn't just me who smelled it! The footage of this experience shows the entire group all holding our shirts or our hands to our mouths and noses, the smell was that overpowering. Unfortunately, these video files have been lost and deleted from YouTube. Yet for those of us who were there, it's something we'll never forget.

This new spirit uttered the Mi'kmaq word *Msit No'kmaq*, which means "all my relations". With that, the spirit who had been trapped disappeared. Just like that.

It was clear to me the spirit who spoke Mi'kmaq, and who put his hand on my back to move me, was a Native Elder from the spirit world. I believe he came to teach me something very important about the power of the light, and about using Native traditions to help lost spirits into the light. It was this experience which later led me to seek out a living Native Elder to teach me more about our traditional ways.

My experiences with the paranormal group taught me a lot about the different realities, or realms, where spirit can reside. I've learned human beings who die don't always embrace the light and move on. Rather, some get stuck in an in-between place, and they have the ability to communicate with us—sometimes in a dramatic fashion! I also learned there are beings of light helping them to move on, and that we all can play a part in facilitating that movement toward the light.

It is my own thirst for knowledge, and deep curiosity about the spirit world, which caused me to go out and have these experiences. The things I learned have made me eager to pass this information on to others. In fact, it's one of my main reasons for writing this book: I want to share the experiences I've had with you, so any wisdom or knowledge I've gained will help you better understand the spirit world. Because guess what? None of us are getting out of here alive, and we're all going to end up in the same place: the spirit world.

My experiences with the paranormal group also introduced me to the amazing fact some voices—like Victoria, but also other spirits—can actually be recorded and captured on a digital recorder. This is a bizarre phenomenon even I don't fully understand. Although, in the moment, no one else could hear their voices but me, have been captured digitally and heard later by others. (If you're interested in hearing some of these voices for yourself, you may find them on my YouTube channel: https://youtu.be/gyaUWjlnXzc.

CHAPTER 16

Connecting at Costco

In my career field, there aren't many of us who are household names. Sylvia Browne is one; Theresa Caputo is another. Known as the Long Island Medium, Caputo became famous for her reality show of the same name. About a year after my first live show in Halifax, I had what I like to call a Theresa Caputo moment; and it happened in a place I certainly never expected. Costco. That's right! Canada's biggest wholesale warehouse store.

It was a warm fall afternoon when I ventured into Costco. I was in a bit of a hurry and only needed a few things, so I resisted the urge to get a cart. (We all know what happens when you get a cart at Costco—you buy too much stuff!) I realized as I stood in line, waiting to pay, that I was hungry. So, with my hands full of the groceries I'd just bought, I found myself in the lineup for a hotdog.

A young man with two young children was standing in front of me. He kept turning around, looking at me, before finally saying, "You're Shawn Leonard."

I didn't recognize him, so I had to ask how we met.

"We didn't actually meet, but I came to your show in Halifax—at the Forum."

I rarely recall the specifics of any readings I do as it's just way too much information to keep in my head, so I asked if I read him.

"Well, you tried," he chuckled, "but I don't think I was ready. You came to my side of the stage and pointed to the area where I was sitting. You said there was a mother figure named Mildred who was trying to make a connection, but I didn't own it."

"Was that your mom's name?"

"It was; I just wasn't ready. That night really opened my eyes, though." The man's food arrived.

"I'm glad," I said. "Thanks for letting me know. Enjoy your lunch."

I assumed that was the end of our interaction, but a few minutes later I was standing, hands still full of groceries but now with a soft drink and hotdog, looking for a place to sit. Wouldn't you know, but the only free table in the entire seating area was with the young man and his two young kids.

I walked over and asked if I could sit with them. He agreed and introduced himself as Dan Glover.

"You know, it's kind of funny I'm running into you today," he said.

I knew there was something up. When the only seat in the food court was next to Dan I figured there was a reason for our meeting. It didn't take long to figure out what was going on. "Why's that?" I asked.

"Well, I'm pretty sure it was my mom who was trying to communicate with you at your show. I just wasn't ready then.

Now today is her birthday, and here I am running into you. Seems like a bit of a coincidence."

"Well, I've learned there are no coincidences." I smiled at him as I began to feel his mother very much around us, trying to get my attention. I was pretty sure she had arranged for us to meet here at Costco. Then I got a very specific piece of information: "Your mom wants you to know you don't need to put anything on her grave. You can just plant something, or have flowers at your house, and she can enjoy them there. She's always with you."

His face blanched. "What did you just say?"

"She doesn't need you to plant anything on her grave."

"How did you know that?" Dan had stopped eating now.

"Your mother is letting me know," I said. "She's right here with you."

"I just planted a blue juniper on her grave, like two days ago," he said. "And when I walked in here today there were five or six employees planting blue junipers outside. I thought it was a bit strange, so I called my wife to tell her." Dan shook his head. "And now you're telling me my mom's right here?"

"That's right," I said, and very quickly other information became apparent; I saw his mother had died in a fire.

"Your mom died in a fire when you were young. She was young, too. Yet she wasn't alone; I can see she was with her sister?"

Dan nodded quietly, agreeing with everything I said. I could practically see the goosebumps erupting on his body.

"She almost got out of the house."

"She did?" Dan hadn't known that piece of information, but later confirmed with an uncle that his mother's body had been found just inside the doorway. Dan was only ten at the time, and had been out with his father when his mother and his aunt had mistakenly set the house on fire. They both perished, but I could see they hadn't suffered.

"Your mom passed out from smoke inhalation," I said. "She was unconscious. She didn't suffer." Suddenly, I felt someone touching my left shoulder. I knew it was Dan's mother, trying to direct my attention to something on her son's left shoulder. I could see it then in my mind's eye: a tattoo! He had a tattoo of his mother's face. Dan had on three-quarter length sleeves, so I couldn't see the tattoo but knew it was there. "She wants you to know she's pretty impressed with that artwork you've got on your shoulder," I said, pointing to where I knew it was.

Dan's entire face crumpled as he broke down, crying hard. Tears streaming down his face he raised his sleeve up over his shoulder to show me his mother's face.

"None of this was an accident, us meeting up today," I said. "Your mom orchestrated all of this. It's her birthday, and we were meant to share this moment so I could give you this message: she loves you, and she knows who your children are. She's very proud of you."

Mildred Glover would have been fifty the day I ran into her son at Costco. There's no doubt that what happened was a tragedy for the family, and very unfortunate. But, I also truly believe Dan would not be able to be the man, and the father, he is today without his mom having passed when he was still so young. While none of us can possibly understand the timing of a loved one's death, I do know there's always a reason for everything. I felt so humbled Mildred had chosen me to deliver her important message to her son. I was so happy she was able to give Dan such solid reassurance. After that day at Costco he knew, without a shadow of a doubt, his mom was always with him and always had been—loving him fiercely and terrifically proud.

CHAPTER 17

A Physical Encounter with My Guides

When you pay attention and you go with the flow of where life wants to take you, it's easy to see our existence here on earth as one *hello* and one *goodbye* after another—and I'm not just talking about death! I'm also referring to the way our situation changes over time, when we listen to our own inner guide and allow ourselves to be directed. We humans seldom stay in the same place for long, energetically speaking, and if we do we quickly become stagnant.

In my own life, I have found this to be true for the people I surround myself with. During the time after my wife and I divorced, but before I started dating again, was no exception. A member of the paranormal group was trying to insinuate herself into my life, and everything about her raised a huge red flag. I left the group, but took the extra step of asking my guides to please do whatever they needed to make sure I didn't ever run into that person again.

They came through on their promise, in a way I never could anticipated. It happened on a day I was downtown delivering the mail. It was early morning and not many people were up and about. In fact, none of the stores were even open. As I turned onto Blowers Street and began heading up the hill toward Halifax's infamous "pizza corner" (frequented by late-night partiers), I came upon an old homeless man sitting on the sidewalk.

I said good morning, but as I passed he grabbed my arm. "Hey, can I talk to you?" he rasped.

My days at Canada Post were winding down, and I was always in a hurry to deliver the mail and get home so I would be fresh and rested for the spirit messages I delivered each night. "Sure, but I can't chat for long," I said, patting the mailbag. "I have to get this stuff delivered."

I tried to follow what he said, but the old man was mostly speaking gibberish. When I told him I had to go and turned to walk away he yelled out, "Do you know Brian at Canada Post?" He didn't wait for a response and just kept talking. It seemed clear the man wanted to keep me there, and certainly wasn't going to let me go willingly.

I find these situations hard, as I never want to appear rude, but I finally interrupted him and said, "I'm really sorry, but I have to go. I'm really grateful you spoke to me, and it was really nice to meet you, but I have to finish my work for today."

Suddenly, he completely relented. Looking me right in the eyes, he said, "Okay, goodbye for now. I'll see you again."

I breathed a sigh of relief and walked up the hill, almost colliding with a very tall man and quite a short woman who were coming around the corner at that exact moment. The tall man got right in my face. He looked familiar in a way I couldn't immediately place.

"I'm not from around here," the tall man said. "My name is Sam, and I'm looking for a place to go eat breakfast."

What the heck? What was the likelihood, on a quiet, early morning, of being approached and chatted up by two separate people within minutes of each other? When I normally walked this route I didn't see a soul.

"Can you tell me a good place to eat breakfast?" he repeated.

Remember the *Seinfeld* episode with the close-talker? That was this guy. He was definitely in my physical space, and every time I tried to inch backward he and his companion crept forward. I stole a glance at her; she looked concerned. Breakfast? I began to think about places that might be open so early. There was the Bluenose II down on Barrington street, and....

The man interrupted my thoughts. "Well, I know the Bluenose II is just down the hill," he said.

I thought he said he wasn't from here? Did he actually say his name was Sam? Why introduce himself just to ask me directions? That felt weird, so I turned my thoughts back to breakfast. There was also Smitty's up on Spring Garden Road across from the public gardens. As soon as I thought this, he again chimed in.

"And then there's Smitty's, up near the public gardens."

I was beginning to feel the goosebumps that come when something unusual, and a little other-worldly, happens. I blurted out, "I thought you weren't from around here?"

Sam leaned in even closer, and said with a smile, "You know what? It's okay. I know where we are going."

And then they walked around me! *What a strange interaction,* I thought. The person whom I had asked for protection from was right in front of me, turning to head uphill and walking the other way. I turned on my heel and did a one hundred and eighty-degree turn. To my astonishment everyone I had just been talking to, and walked past me, had completely vanished! The tall man and his concerned companion were gone, as was the homeless man on the sidewalk. All had completely disappeared. I shook my head. They had just been here; literally only seconds had passed.

In that moment I put all the pieces together. I suddenly knew Sam and Victoria had actually taken physical form to help me avoid the person who I intuitively felt wanted to cause me trouble. Sam had even named himself, which explained why he looked familiar! I realized they were delaying me. Had they not, I would have run right into the woman from my paranormal group. They were helping me, doing what I asked them to. After, I replayed the situation in my mind hundreds of times, wanting to understand the timing. Why then and not another time? Did they know something I didn't about what may have happened had I run into that woman?

I remain immensely grateful for their intervention, and my brief encounter with them in physical form. I would love for it to happen again—my guides appearing within human bodies to help me—and have asked for the awareness to really appreciate the next time it happens!

CHAPTER 18

My First Eagle Feather

One of the joys of being back in Nova Scotia was the opportunity to immerse myself in the beautiful landscape where I grew up. Along with a few old friends, I started an annual tradition of kayaking down the Shubenacadie River, from Enfield to Elmsdale. One year, not long after my experience of being aided by the Native Elder in spirit form on McNabs Island, my friends and I were out for our kayak down the river. It was a beautiful day, and as I drifted out ahead of the rest I noticed an eagle sitting in a tree. It looked young, and I intuitively felt it was a female.

She watched as I kayaked by. I was maybe three or four hundred feet past when suddenly she flew right over my head. I heard her before I saw her, and goosebumps erupted over my body as I watched her land very close by in another tree. She continued to watch me, and then did the same thing again;

waited until I had passed before sweeping right over top of the kayak and landing in another tree.

Since my encounter with the spirit on McNabs Island I'd done a little reading about proper smudging, and knew the process involved an eagle feather. I had also found out these feathers must be given to the person who uses them. This eagle's close proximity, as well as the sense she was watching and following me, made me wonder if an eagle feather was coming to me that day.

With this in mind, I spoke to her as she flew over me for the third and fourth time. *"Kitpu,"* (pronounced *Git-pu*) I said out loud, voice raised. It was the Mi'kmaq word for eagle. "I would appreciate an eagle feather. I've been looking for one, but haven't found any. Is there a way you could give me one? Because I could use one for the work I do."

Nothing happened. I was still ahead of the others, and as I paddled further down the river she did it again. And again. And again. Each time she flew so close to my head I could feel wings graze my hair. Finally, after about the tenth swoop over top of me and my boat, a feather dropped from the sky and landed in the water. I raced like crazy to get it.

She was watching from a nearby tree as I finally reached into the water and fished it out. There was a little crick in it with a piece missing. I had been hoping for a large, magnificent eagle feather, but what I got was a smaller, not-so-perfect one. Do you know what I had the nerve to say? I looked up at her and asked, "Do you have a better feather?" She had stayed steadfastly with me all the way down the river, but when I uttered that question she took one look at me and flew off. I didn't see her again for the rest of the day. At the time I didn't really know much about Native culture, so I didn't know that I should have thanked the eagle, in Mi'kmaq, for her gift. I should have said, *"Wela'lin, Kitpu,* for your gift." I don't blame the eagle for flying away!

Since then, I've learned so much about Native traditions. I've learned the eagle is sacred because it flies the highest, and therefore comes closest to the creator. In the Mi'kmaq creation story, the eagle flies above all the storms, and all the negativity and darkness of the world. When an eagle descends to earth to help you, and gifts you a feather, it is a high honour.

Despite having received many other eagle feathers since then, this first is still very special to me. I honour it and know it was meant for me. I am so grateful for each feather gifted during my life; and they have all helped me clear and move energy with clients.

If you are meant to be a healer I believe an eagle feather will come to you. Talk to our source, our creator, and even to the eagles themselves, and ask for your feather. Eagle feathers can help us all through our darkest times. If you use an eagle feather to heal others, or clear their energy, it is a great gift indeed.

CHAPTER 19

The Big Nudge

Within a couple of years after arriving in Nova Scotia I was booking clients six months in advance, doing a dozen or more readings per week, and organizing live shows. Despite the success of being able to start from scratch in a new place, and the way people just seemed to find me without any advertising, I still felt compelled to hang onto my Canada Post job—with its steady pay, benefits, and pension.

My guides were patient with me, continually reminding me as to what my real calling was, and reinforcing the message it was safe to leave my nine-to-five job. Yet I simply couldn't do it. The fear of not having enough money to pay my own bills and living expenses, plus my child and spousal support, paralyzed me.

I continued to ignore these messages to the point I now see the spirits had to step in with a stronger message; one I wouldn't be able to ignore. My body broke down. It took some major physical hardship for me to learn it's easier to just let go and trust. I tell you this story with the hope you will not let fear control your life, or your choices.

It started with a tear in my meniscus in my left knee, which led to multiple knee surgeries. As I was trying to heal I herniated the L3-L4 disk in my back, which was excruciatingly painful. I had to use a wheelchair, and was unable to work at all for a time. I was on a waiting list for back surgery, and due to the strong painkillers I even had to suspend my readings for clients. It was a dark time. I went to the chiropractor's, laser therapy, physiotherapy, and acupuncture. I did everything I could, but for a while it felt like nothing helped.

Slowly, I started to heal. Although I was still reliant on a wheelchair, and able to do readings, I found I had developed a new clarity. I realized these physical challenges were serving as the big nudge I needed to make some necessary changes. I developed a new inner strength, as well as an increased psychic strength during this time. It was apparent I was even more accurate and tuned in when I wasn't exhausted from working a physically demanding full-time job.

Even as I made the decision to quit, I still had a lot of fear. Yet I also felt enormously supported by the universe—and relieved I had finally done it. Everything came together and continued to flow. As I healed, and no longer had another job to go to, I was able to do even more readings and shows. I even chose not to have the back surgery, and started practising yoga to strengthen my core and stay grounded.

Letting go of our fears can be very difficult, but necessary. I learned the hard way it's best to deal with the fear and leave unhealthy situations—whether at work or in relationships. I hope your path to this realization is easier!

CHAPTER 20

An Elder Appears

As I developed and grew as a medium, and became better known in Nova Scotia, there came opportunities to donate my services to worthwhile causes. In 2013, Veith House, a non-profit organization in Halifax, asked me to give a free evening of readings. I was happy to do it, and certainly had no idea how significantly my life would change afterward.

The audience was small enough—about fifty people—for me to connect with almost everybody in the room, even if only for a short time. There was a Mi'kmaq woman sitting in the front row with another, younger woman, who looked as though she might be her daughter. When I connected with the older woman an important piece of information was immediately delivered.

"The spirit world is telling me very clearly you've recently heard about four Indigenous people who were missing, murdered. I think this was in the Cape Breton area. I see a large body of water, perhaps the Bras d'Or Lake area, and a hill leading up from the water. I believe there is a person named Joe connected to the story. If you figure out who Joe is, tell him I know where their remains are. Do you know anything about this?"

She and her daughter exchanged a quick look. "I just learned of this story yesterday," the older woman said. "I met with someone who told me about it."

The information was coming fast and I knew it was important. "I have a feeling you're a writer, or some kind of storyteller, and there is a calling for you to somehow put this story out there."

She thanked me and I moved on, but after the night ended the two women stayed in my mind. Up to that point I hadn't had much opportunity to read people from my own culture. In fact, that event marked the first time I had ever connected so strongly with somebody who was also Mi'kmaq. I had a feeling the Great Spirit was in the midst of answering a prayer I had put out there after my experience on McNabs Island, when the Native Elder from the spirit world had appeared. This encounter made me hunger for a connection with a living Mi'kmaq Elder; one who could teach me more about Native traditions.

Sure enough, the woman from the night at Veith House contacted me privately. We became friends, and, over time, I told her I was looking for a mentor. She told me there was someone I should meet, and before I knew it there was a Mi'kmaq Elder standing on my doorstep, holding something in his arms. I was soon to learn he was carrying a "bundle," which contained a sacred eagle wing along with the traditional medicines of sage, sweetgrass, tobacco, and cedar.

"I heard you want to learn about traditional ways," he said.

I invited him in, and made him a cup of tea. We settled in my office, where I did client readings, for our chat. I told him although I was Mi'kmaq I hadn't been raised knowing any traditional practices. The Elder placed the bundle on the table and unwrapped it. The first thing I noticed was the enormous eagle wing, stitched with very fine beadwork.

"I see you have some feathers." He pointed to ones which adorned my office. I noticed the Elder chose his words carefully, and never said more than what was required. He went on to tell me feathers were gifts from the Great Spirit, and taught me how to respect these gifts by handling them in the right way. During that first visit he also showed me how to do proper smudging, in addition to teaching me some Mi'kmaq words. As he left he invited me to be part of a couple of upcoming events, including a sweat lodge ceremony.

As the Elder continued to teach me in the traditional ways, and expose me to Mi'kmaq culture, he was also subtly checking me out. He came to a few of my events, saw the work I was doing, and came to believe in my gift. He even said he saw me as a spiritual healer.

As we worked together, it became clear the murdered Aboriginal people I felt in the reading at Veith House were the Elder's relatives. I tentatively broached the subject one day, and asked if he was interested in hearing what information I was being sent via the spirit world. He was open to the experience, and I was able to provide some details about how his relatives had died, and at whose hands. I further asked if he would like my help locating their bodies, as I already had a feeling I knew where they were.

He accepted my offer of help and together with my friend Doug, who owns a cadaver dog, we travelled to Big Pond, Cape Breton. We searched the area where I felt his relatives bodies were buried, and Doug's dog, Breya, indicated an area under a tree which was probably over fifty years old. Doug had brought another friend who owned a search and rescue dog, and her dog also indicated the same location. I felt satisfied knowing I may have given the Elder some sort of closure with my information, as well as a location of his relatives bodies. This felt like my way of thanking him for his teachings.

We shared many special moments over the years he served as my teacher and guide. One of my proudest moments came when the Elder gave me my Mi'kmaq name: Wape'k Kitpu Aknutmajik Jijaqmijk (White Eagle Spirit Talker). During the year which preceded the gift of my name, I had found three, pure-white eagle tail feathers. I don't think this was an accident; it felt like everything was coming together.

Later, the Elder also gifted me with a walking stick on which my new Mi'kmaq name was written. Yet perhaps the biggest honour he bestowed upon me was the gift of his eagle wing, which I had seen on the day of our very first visit. It had been given to him by an Elder who had taught him many years before, and tradition dictated he pass this wing on to a student when a new wing entered his life. This had just happened; the Elder had been gifted a new wing from a local wildlife park and decided I would be the recipient of the one he had carried for years.

He told me I should use this wing to heal people and clear their energy. Then he taught me how to properly smudge using this sacred object and spiritual medicines. He also instructed I keep it wrapped inside the bundle, which was made of a red cloth, to keep it protected and clear from outside energies.

I felt very honoured by this sacred gift, and carry it with me when I travel for events, using the wing to smudge the room where everyone will gather. I also use it during any of my sessions where a client may be going through a particularly hard time. I know smudging them with the wing will help them move, or release, some of the energy they're carrying.

Someday, when I become an Elder and share the teachings, and when a new wing comes into my life, I will pass on this eagle wing to another on their journey.

CHAPTER 21

The Importance of Validation

When people come to see a medium what they're looking for is evidence their loved one still exists, and are perhaps hoping some contact can be established. I call this "validation," and I take it very, very seriously. I have become known for the accuracy of the names I am able to provide for people. Not all mediums receive names from the spirit world, so I consider myself to be quite fortunate. Sometimes I hear names quite clearly, and other times I receive images which help paint a picture.

Such was the case with a young woman who came to see me, looking to connect with her grandmother. This happened quickly and easily, and I was able to give the young woman all kinds of specific information, including how and when her grandmother died. Yet I could tell the woman was waiting for something else, something very specific. Just then, an unusual image popped into my mind, one I'd not seen before. It was a glass of milk, and a saucer with three cookies.

"I have to ask you something. Your grandma is showing me milk and cookies on a plate. Does that mean anything to you?"

The young woman replied no, she didn't know what the image meant. I tried to move on, but it was like the grandmother wouldn't let me. She kept repeating the same image: milk and cookies, milk and cookies, over and over.

"Are you sure?" I asked again. "She just keeps reiterating this milk and cookies on a plate thing, and she's not giving up. She's being really insistent."

All of a sudden the young woman sat right up and shouted, "Oh my God! Cookie! You got it!"

"Sorry?" Although my client seemed very happy by what had just happened, I was still mystified.

"Before I came today I asked my grandma to send her nickname because it's something no one else knows. Her nickname was Cookie! Now, I *know* it's her."

For me, this was an excellent example of having to trust what appears, and also a reminder to be patient while the client catches up with their relative in the spirit world. The grandmother knew her granddaughter needed to hear the word "cookie," and she did her best to get me to say it repeatedly!

Validation can also come in the form of memories or experiences which no one else but the person sitting in front of me and their deceased loved one could possibly know. One of the most startling examples of this occurred a few years ago. Jessica was a young seventeen-year-old, who passed away suddenly from an undiagnosed heart condition. Her parents made an appointment and Jessica began communicating with me in earnest, telling me information about her passing, asking me to tell her parents she was okay and she loved them.

It was then something very unusual happened; something I never expected to experience. Jessica gave me an image of herself in a bra, and had been quite a large-breasted young woman. This was very awkward. I make a point of trusting everything I receive from spirit and voicing what I see, even if I don't understand. This, however, seemed terribly inappropriate. How do you tell two grieving parents their daughter just showed up in only a bra? I took a deep breath and began by apologizing.

"I want you to know how sorry I am about your daughter's passing." I paused and cleared my throat. "Sometimes people who have passed will show me unexpected things I don't understand. Your daughter is showing me something which feels awkward, but I trust it's for a reason and you will understand."

They looked at me expectantly.

"Your daughter is appearing to me in only a bra." I felt terribly embarrassed, and could feel my face turning red. "I can see she is quite large-breasted, and there is something very significant about the bra I am supposed to talk to you about."

Imagine my relief when their jaws nearly hit the floor and they began laughing. But their laughter soon turned to tears as the reality of their daughter's presence was vividly confirmed. "It's her. It's definitely her," they said, nodding vigorously and clutching each other's hands. They went on to tell me how their daughter had often been teased, especially by her sister who called her Big Boobs. On the first anniversary of Jessica's passing the family got everyone together to celebrate Jessica's life, for which they did a unique activity. They bedazzled one of Jessica's bras in honour of her memory, decorating it with all things bright and sparkling.

This is why it had been important for Jessica to show

me her bra. It was a piece of unique information no one else but close family and friends could have known. This isn't something you would post on Facebook. This isn't something you would write on a blog. This was the thing Jessica knew would allow her parents to believe she was still there and still with them, just no longer in physical form.

The last story I will share in this chapter is also a very unique one, which involves a famous deceased person appearing in a vision during a client session. A woman who hadn't booked under her own name, and who seemed quite suspicious, had come to see me. She didn't tell me with whom she was trying to connect, but someone came through right away. It was a young man who I felt had taken his own life. I sensed he had been her boyfriend. He apologized to her for what had happened, and told her it wasn't her fault. He talked about having been depressed and on drugs, and encouraged her to find her way in life. He said although he hadn't been mentally well in life, he was healthy and happy in the spirit world and had finally found peace. He then showed me an image of himself onstage with a microphone, and he did look really good—vibrant and healthy. Suddenly, a guy walked out from behind him and it was Tupac Shakur, the famous rapper who had also passed away. The guy put his arm around Tupac, and there they stood together in front of the mic.

"I'm not sure why I'm getting this, but your boyfriend is showing me an image of himself on a stage with Tupac Shakur. You know who I mean? The rapper guy who died?" She certainly did know who I meant!

"Oh my God! Are you freaking kidding me?!" she yelled, jumping up off the couch. She then yanked off her hoodie and hauled up the back of her t-shirt. There, covering her entire back, was an enormous tattoo of Tupac Shakur. "Do you see that?" she asked, excited. "My boyfriend and I both loved

Tupac, so we got matching tattoos. He had the exact same one on his back."

She went on to tell me she had thought the whole medium thing was not real, or possible. That was why she hadn't booked under her real name, so I couldn't find out any information before our session. "But there's no way you could have known about Tupac," she said. "And I know you didn't see it. I was wearing a hoodie the whole time." Suddenly, the reality of knowing her boyfriend was right there, communicating with her, overwhelmed her and she broke down in tears. "It's really him. Tell him I love him. I still love him so much."

"And he loves you," I assured.

These three stories are just a small sampling of the amazing ways in which the spirit communicates. Some days I can hardly believe I am lucky enough to have been given this ability to act as a bridge between this and the spirit world. Being able to provide this kind of comfort, as well as being able to help heal grieving hearts, is a true gift.

CHAPTER 22

Courageous Parents

Many different people reach out to mediums in order to connect with loved ones who have passed, but perhaps the saddest encounters are with those who are grieving a child who has crossed over into the light from suicide. The readings where a parent has lost a child are always very difficult. I couldn't imagine dealing with such a loss, even knowing what I know.

If you are reading this book, and have lost a child to suicide, the most important thing I want you to know is the dogmatic, religious ideas about what happens to someone who takes their own life are not true. No matter how we die, we all end up in the same place—within the love and light of the spirit world. Know your child is safe and loved and happy and healthy, and they are able to communicate with you from where they are now.

On the other hand, if you are reading this book and you're

someone who is tempted to take your own life, please, seek help! Ask for help! I implore you to consider there is always hope for a better life, and there are always other options. I know this because I've received this information from many spirits. From their new vantage point they are able to offer helpful information on what can be done if you are struggling.

When someone who has taken their own life comes through during a reading, usually the first thing they express is regret. They are not only sad about the pain they have caused to the people who love them, but they've all repeatedly told me they wished they had sought more help; they wished they would have talked to one more person. Without exception, they all say they were so focused on the issues, on what was wrong in their lives, there seemed no room for solutions.

Many have even sent images of themselves in a room, facing one particular wall, but are not able to shift their body, their feet seemingly frozen in place. On the wall they are facing are all the problems, all the negative thoughts and experiences they've ever had. They show me how they were completely focused on that wall, unable to turn around and see the wall on the other side of the room is full of hope, solutions, and love for themselves. They have shown me all that was required to heal was a pivot, a shifting of the heart and the mind toward this different way of looking at things. As the late Wayne Dyer said, "If you change the way you look at things, the things you look at change."

They acknowledge that as a human being this shift is extremely hard, but from their new perspective in a place made of only light and love, they can see there was indeed a way out of the things which were weighing them down. They tell me the ability to overcome and to refocus was always within—they just didn't know it. For people who have taken their own lives the strongest message I receive is always this: "There was another way; I just couldn't see it then."

Alexis was a seventeen-year-old girl who struggled for a few months before being diagnosed with biological, chemical depression. This was only a few days before she took her own life in December of 2015. Her mother, Bev Fletcher, came to see me for a reading. I was able to connect with Alexis right away, and while she told me she had absolutely found the peace she so deeply desired she also now realized there were other options available—but she couldn't see them while alive. Through me, Alexis told her mother she was working behind the scenes, as a motivating force for the non-profit foundation her mom had created.

Knowing her daughter is supporting her has fuelled Bev's work on Believe in Hope, the organization she founded to raise awareness about mental illness and suicide prevention in adolescents. She works hard to raise funds which go toward early prevention, mental health education, and training for teachers and/or parents, as well as coping skills enhancement, and peer support and anti-stigma initiatives.

Rehtaeh Parsons was another seventeen-year-old young woman who took her own life. She had been sexually assaulted, only to then be ostracized by her community through an elaborate cyber-bullying campaign created by those who assaulted her. After her death, this Nova Scotian story became international news and her mother, Leah Parsons, became the voice Rehtaeh never had. Leah shared her daughter's story to advocate for change within the educational, medical, police, and legal systems which failed her daughter.

On the day Leah came to see me I knew something was up right away. At the start of every reading I record the date and the time. "Today's date is the fourth of April, 4:04 p.m.," I said into the digital recorder. *That's odd,* I thought. It was the fourth minute of the fourth hour of the fourth day of the fourth month. I knew right away it couldn't be a coincidence. When things lineup like that, or when there are unusual synchronicities, I know there is a message or a meaning behind it.

"Is this day important to you?" I asked, and Leah silently nodded. She later told me when she booked the appointment my only available slot was on the anniversary of her daughter's death: April 4.

As soon as our reading began, Rehtaeh quickly showed herself to me and I recognized her from media photos. I felt comfortable asking Leah outright if Rehtaeh Parsons was her daughter.

I could see Rehtaeh was a beautiful, bright light, with a lot of love in her heart. She communicated her regret over her choice to take her own life, but was helping her mother in her new role as activist. I could also see Rehtaeh wasn't alone in the spirit world. She was with someone named Anne or Annie, who Leah confirmed was Rehtaeh's late grandmother.

I have been incredibly moved by the stories of Rehtaeh Parsons's and Alexis Fletcher's families; these parents are not only healing from, and dealing with, such a tragic loss, but they've also taken it upon themselves to speak out and raise awareness so other families may be spared what they continue to endure.

The earth can be a hard place with a lot of struggle and pain. One of the messages I consistently receive from the spirit world is people who have taken their own lives were often not aware of the amount of love and care available to them. So, I like to share this message as broadly as I can: to anyone reading this book I encourage you to take time and notice your friends, notice your family. Talk to them, and ask how they are; tell them you love them. If you are someone who is suffering, reach out to people and talk to someone who cares. Get the help you need. Don't give up and don't look back unless you are doing so to forgive. Do your best to let go of painful situations and experiences.

I pray everyone who reads this book will find the strength and courage to look at the other wall, the one all about love and hope. If you're constantly focusing your mind on what's wrong, you'll never find the solution nor the answer nor the peace you desperately seek. It doesn't matter how far the path is, or how long it takes for you to get there; what matters is you're looking forward and moving in the right direction. Thought patterns and toxic beliefs can be changed through the power of our own minds. Choosing a new focus can change, and maybe even save, a life. Learning to find love, and to be loving toward yourself and others, is what life is all about.

For further assistance:
Canada Suicide Prevention Service (CSPS)
Callers anywhere in Canada can access crisis support using the technology of their choice (phone, text, or chat), in French or English:
Phone: 1-833-456-4566 (toll-free) **Text:** 45645
Chat: crisisservicescanada.ca **Web:** http://thelifelinecanada.ca/

Kids Help Phone: 1-800-668-6868
(Ages 20 years and under)

First Nations and Inuit Hope for Wellness, 24/7 Help Line: 1-855-242-3310

Canadian Indian Residential Schools Crisis Line:
1-866-925-4419

Trans LifeLine: 1-877-330-6366
(all ages)

USA National Suicide Prevention Lifeline
Phone: 1-800-273-8255
Web: https://suicidepreventionlifeline.org/
Believe in Hope: https://believeinhopeforalexis.com/
Rehtaeh Parsons Society: http://rehtaehparsons.ca/

CHAPTER 23

An Unexpected Voice

This is the part of the book where I want to assure you just because someone is a psychic doesn't mean they make the right decisions all the time. I've made more than my fair share of mistakes, and I've also actively ignored guidance from the spirit realm. The longer I live the more I believe wisdom really comes from sometimes making bad choices. In my case, I'm grateful for the difficult and hard learning experiences I've had because I know I can use these lessons to help others.

Case in point: a while after Marissa and I broke up, I met someone and we started dating. Although there were many red flags I managed to ignore them all. I am really good at ignoring the signs for myself. I always feel I can find a way through relationship struggles even though it isn't a healthy relationship. I was eventually able to leave the relationship, but not before a lot of drama ensued. Being psychic didn't keep me from making mistakes, and I've come to believe I needed to face these specific struggles in order to grow and learn how to cultivate a greater love for myself.

Through it all guidance from the spirits was literally being dropped at my feet. It was lodged in my gut every day, but I ignored it. I was conscious of not wanting to have another relationship fail, and I truly thought if I just tried harder this relationship would work. I had all the solutions. I am extremely patient and loving to my detriment, especially with a partner to whom I have chosen to give my heart.

The truth is there is all kinds of guidance available to us at all times—it's just that very few of us know how to access it, while others (like me) can be quite good at ignoring it. Our guides communicate with us in so many ways; through our intuition, our feelings, or our gut sense something is off or wrong. We always have the choice whether or not to listen, but they are always on our side.

Throughout my life I've also felt the guiding hand of my father, and occasionally have felt the presence of someone who was well-known during their time on earth, yet who have passed on. This has happened with the famous writer Wayne Dyer (see next chapter), and even, but only once, with Jesus. I'm quite aware writing these words may alienate some readers, but I'm willing to do so because I feel it's important everyone reading this understand there are many sources of wisdom available to each and every one of us.

Let me first say I don't consider the Bible to be the word of God, and I don't actually believe in the Biblical Jesus. Rather, I believe in a much different, all-loving teacher and healer who was put on the earth to help us. I believe Jesus was a human being who understood, and used, his connection to the creator or God or the Great Spirit (or whichever word you want to use for the infinite energy of love). It's the same connection to which we all have access, but most of us don't know this. I believe Jesus was a very spiritual person who healed people, who died for his beliefs, and who was willing to do all that because he knew no matter what happened both he and his message would live on.

My encounter with Jesus happened one morning as I was lying in bed, after a hurtful incident the night before. My children were not thrilled I was with this new person and I had sent them an email explaining my stance. I was struggling emotionally. I didn't want my children to dislike my partner, or ruin the possibility of them having a relationship with her. Of course, I was also terribly worried I wouldn't be able to mend this issue with my children.

I was unable to sleep and could hear my guides trying to insert themselves in my thoughts, but I wasn't open to listening. Just then, a loud voice within my mind sounded clear. "Shun." It was just this one word, which I recognized as my name laced with a distinct Jewish accent.

I don't hear loud voices very often, so it took me by surprise. I lay in stunned silence. A minute later, the voice repeated my name. "Shun!"

This time I answered. "Yes?" I immediately heard this message, loud and clear: "Shun, you do not have a bad family; you have a good family!"

I had never heard another voice like it, before or since, and I had never felt so much love and compassion from any other spirit voice. Even today, when I think of the sound of the voice and what he said, it's easy for me to well up with emotion.

When I heard that voice I knew my guides had got the man known as Jesus to talk to me, as I wasn't listening to them and they knew I was really struggling. The one simple sentence he shared, delivered with so much love, compassion, and wisdom, changed me. And it changed how I felt. It didn't necessarily change the situation, but it enabled me to know somehow, with time, all would work itself out. And it has.

Having heard the voice on that particular day made me wish I had heard it sooner. I wish I had known I was able to hear the voice of Jesus. Hearing that one sentence taught me so much: I know he's there and I know he's a connection point to the creator—in the same way as my guides.

After this experience I remembered conversations Sam and I would have when I was a kid. I remember things he said about who Jesus really was, and I had another look at my notes from my days with the Novus Spiritus Church. I read with interest that Jesus was likely not his actual name. Rather it is thought it was Joshua, which in Arabic and Hebrew would have been pronounced Yeshua—Joshua.

I think of the man who spoke to me as Joshua, and even though I don't feel as though he's one of my guides he definitely guided me that day. I'm convinced we all have access to him, and he's there for all of us. By no means am I saying everyone should go to church; I don't think you're going to find God in a church anyway.

Rather, God is within all of us. It's a connection we all carry inside our hearts. I want to encourage you to trust any loving voices which come through. That infinite, divine love is there for all of us, at any time. We just need an open heart, and open mind, to hear it.

CHAPTER 24

Dreams and Gabriel

I wanted to visit Charlottetown, Prince Edward Island for a self-produced event at the Rodd Charlottetown Hotel. I love this venue because of its history; it was built in 1931 by the Canadian National Railway. It was a smaller venue, and a very intimate experience. The event went well, with roughly ninety per cent of the audience staying after for pictures and to ask questions. I felt very happy being able to validate the spirit messages I was being sent.

After everybody left I gathered all my sound equipment and personal belongings and walked out of the room. I noticed a dime on the floor, which quickly grabbed my attention. The strange thing was I had just walked right by and had not seen it. I felt my father was with me, and I acknowledged it—feeling as though he attended my event that evening and was proud of me. With a smile I put the dime in my pocket.

Feeling tired and grateful, my partner and I headed to our room on the fifth floor. We had not been there until now, and she went in before me as I was pushing our luggage through the doorway. I had left one suitcase just outside the door, and I wanted to grab it as quickly as I could. When I opened the door I was surprised to see a five-dollar bill sitting perfectly flat on top of the suitcase. I grabbed it and placed it in my pocket, scanning up and down the hall for other people. *Strange*, I thought to myself. *Perhaps my dad is trying to tell me something.*

I quickly fell asleep and slipped into a dark dream I've had several times. The dream is typically dark and fearful. There is a cloaked older woman in the room where I lay awake in my dream, and she is holding me down on the bed. I try to push her off me, feeling as though she is sitting on my chest, sucking out my life energy. (Not one of my favourite dreams!) It always ends the same: I am trying to push her off until I finally relax and surround myself with light, which I blow into her face. She immediately dissipates. I wake-up, still blowing air out of my mouth, frightened until I realize it was just a dream. I have had this dream for about twenty years.

At 3:00 a.m. I instantly jump up out of bed and begin to pace the room, thinking about my dad visiting and leaving me signs. I decided to smudge myself and the room. I prayed and spoke to the Great Spirit, my guides, and my father to not allow the dream to once again occur after I fall asleep.

The thing is, I've had readings with people who describe similar dreams. I've also read extensively about this dream experience, and have discovered many people have an issue with sleep paralysis. In Newfoundland, my Mi'kmaq grandmother called this dark spirit The Old Hag. My guides have explained she isn't negative at all, and rather is a spirit whose sole purpose is to make sure our own spirits don't get stuck in the astral dream world while we're in this in-between state. Our spirit body gets pushed back into our physical body if we wake before our spirit returns. Hence, seeing and feeling as if that Old Hag is sitting on my chest, holding me down.

My guides have told me to allow them to help facilitate a clean exit, and entrance, back into my body from the dream and astral world. Which I hastened to do after this last experience! I fell quickly back to sleep, and my dreams were now different. I began to see, and feel, myself surrounded by light. In the room was a man around thirty years old, wearing a long white robe, and with short, black curly hair. As he walked up to me he seemed radiant, glowing with light.

"Shawn," he said, "I want you to know you will soon be going through a very difficult and dark time. I want you to know I am going to be with you, and will help protect you through it all."

"Who are you?" I asked. "Are you a new spirit guide? I do not recognize you."

"My name is Gabriel," he replied. "I am like a spirit guide, but I am not. Remember, I am with you and will help you."

I woke up at 7:00 a.m., and explained to my partner the new dream I had, asking what she thought it meant. She didn't know. I called a Mi'kmaq Elder on our way back to Nova Scotia. I wanted to see if he could meet and discuss the dreams and sequence of events. I met the Elder at a Tim Horton's near the Halifax International Airport.

He was alarmed when I told him everything, and explained Gabriel was an angel, a messenger from God and the Great Spirit. The Elder believed Gabriel had been sent to me in preparation for something negative which was about to disrupt my life. I was surprised I met the angel Gabriel, although confused as to why I didn't know he was an angel. I didn't see any wings! I have never seen, nor met, an angel of light before, yet I knew he was wise, loving, and compassionate, and made me feel I would be safe during whatever was coming. The Elder told me to pray, meditate, and smudge regularly, and said he would do a pipe ceremony as soon as he could.

One month after the event in Prince Edward Island, and the dreams, the ongoing relationship issues with my partner ended. Relationships sometimes end; people come into your life for a season, a reason, or sometimes a lifetime.

Still, I needed further guidance and called a dear friend and soul sister, Anne Bérubé

CHAPTER 25

Guidance from the Masters

Guidance doesn't only come from the spirit world; it can also come through people who are living. The Elder who taught me so much, and propelled me further down my spiritual path, is an example of someone living who played a huge role in my growth. That Elder, unbeknownst to him, also reintroduced me to someone else who would become hugely important.

Her name is Anne Bérubé, and she has played a big role as I've learned to trust myself in both my relationships and my profession. We first met when she came to me for a reading many years ago, but crossed paths again in Moncton in 2015 at a Mi'kmaq ceremonial healing and talking circle. It was held at the home of the wife of one of three RCMP officers who had recently been shot and killed.

The minute I saw Anne I knew our meeting again wasn't an accident. In fact, she was in the midst of producing an event for another psychic and asked if I wanted to come as her guest. I didn't know it at the time, but Anne and her company, Autopoetic Ideas, had been responsible for bringing James Van Praagh, Anita Moorjani, Deepak Chopra and Wayne Dyer to the Maritimes. As we got to know each other, it became a bit of a no-brainer we would also work together in the future.

Anne is a Hay House author and a spiritual coach who travels around the world speaking about embodied spirituality. The messages we share very much complement each other, so Anne and I began planning, and speaking at, events together. Over time, I learned one of Anne's early mentors was the late Wayne Dyer. The two had been close friends, as well as business associates, and Anne missed him terribly. On one occasion she even asked if I felt I could connect with him. It wasn't hard; he came through with a clear message, appearing for her as a butterfly, which seemed to confirm something he had already told her. I was incredibly honoured Wayne Dyer, a human being I had long admired for his inspirational words and work, would make himself available to me from the spirit world.

In late 2016, while I was going through a terrible time after the break-up of my relationship, Anne was there for me. She made time to meet for a few hours at a local café, and I can honestly say her support changed the trajectory of my life. Being able to be open and honest and vulnerable with Anne, and having her reflect back to me what she saw happening in my relationship was invaluable. She gave me soulful advice and guidance, and validated all the gut feelings I had ever had about the relationship yet chose to ignore. I'm sure my spirit guides were cheering for joy the day I met with Anne!

At some point during our talk we both became aware we were not alone. Both of us keenly felt Wayne Dyer's presence, and I could sense him, leaning with both elbows on the table, devouring our entire conversation, and delighting in it.

Suddenly, he presented the image of a butterfly. I thought I understood it, based on what she had told me before about the butterfly being his sign, but this time Wayne was showing me a butterfly tattoo, telling me it was on Anne's ribs. Of course, I would have no way of knowing whether or not she had a tattoo, but he was insistent and so I asked. A tear rolled down her cheek as she nodded, yes. Wayne knew this, and had given me this piece of information as confirmation. The fact her dear friend acknowledged the tattoo was very significant to Anne because Wayne had only learned of it the very last time she saw him alive. At the time they discussed how important the symbol of the butterfly was to them both.

Wayne followed up with another image, quick on the heels of the butterfly. It was of him eating carrots out of a little white bowl as he listened to Anne and I talk. I was curious. "Anne, I don't know what this means, but I'm getting this really clear image of Wayne sitting here with us and eating a bowl of carrots."

Anne let out a little gasp and grew teary once more. She explained the last time she and Wayne had shared that same meal together they had been with a large group. Although Wayne and Anne shared a passion for healthy food, Wayne also had a weakness for certain junk foods. That night, when some hot, crispy fries arrived at the table to share Wayne dived right in, but Anne had slapped his hand and said, "Eat your carrots!"

She felt he was teasing her about having been so motherly toward him with this memory. Anne knew Wayne had high cholesterol, and was worried about his health. She admitted she had a bit of guilt; that if she knew Wayne was going to cross over into the spirit world so soon she would have let him eat the fries.

The kind of validations which come from the spirit world continue to amaze and delight. This was a perfect example of receiving a piece of information, in this case one which no one but Anne could possibly know. It also showed Wayne's sense of humour: he was giving Anne a hard time about the carrot incident, but was also acknowledging she had been watching out for him.

That night, when I returned home, I felt better than I had in months, and truly believed I had been guided by two masters: one living and one passed. I was honoured Wayne Dyer had been engaged in our conversation, and I could sense he was really there to try and help. I felt a genuine caring coming from his spirit.

The next day I had a client scheduled for noon. It was one of my last appointments before Christmas, and the woman I was scheduled to meet had brought me a little present. I had never met her before and thought this such a kind gesture, especially considering so much was currently unravelling in my life. The gift was presented in a small Christmas bag, which contained three chocolates and an orange. I held the orange in my hands, immediately understanding its meaning, but the look on my face must have been misunderstood by my client.

"I'm sorry," she said. "I made cookies yesterday, but all I kept hearing and feeling was that I should bring you an orange. I have no idea why, but it's not a very good Christmas gift, is it?"

"It's the best gift you could have given me," I assured her, and went on to ask if she knew who Wayne Dyer was? She had heard of him, but didn't know the story of how he often brought one prop on stage during his live shows: an orange. Wayne used the orange to share an important lesson with his audience. This is Wayne, in his own words, explaining the metaphor of the orange:

I was preparing to speak at an I Can Do It conference, and I decided to bring an orange on stage with me as a prop for my lecture. I opened a conversation with a bright young fellow of about twelve who was sitting in the front row.

"If I were to squeeze this orange as hard as I could, what would come out?" I asked him.

He looked at me like I was a little crazy and said, "Juice, of course."

"Do you think apple juice could come out of it?"

"No!" He laughed.

"What about grapefruit juice?"

"No!"

"What would come out of it?"

"Orange juice, of course."

"Why? Why when you squeeze an orange does orange juice come out?"

He may have been getting a little exasperated with me at this point. "Well, it's an orange and that's what's inside."

I nodded. "Let's assume that this orange isn't an orange, but it's you. And someone squeezes you, puts pressure on you, says something you don't like, offends you. And out of you comes anger, hatred, bitterness, fear. Why? The answer, as our young friend has told us, is because that's what's inside."

It's one of the great lessons in life. What comes out when life squeezes you? When someone hurts or offends you? If anger, pain, and fear come out of you, it's because that's what's inside. It doesn't matter who does the squeezing—your mother, your brother, your children, your boss, your ex-wife. If someone says something about you that you don't like, what comes out of you is what's inside. And what's inside is up to you, it's your choice.

When someone puts the pressure on you and out of you comes anything other than love, it's because that's what you've allowed to be inside. Once you take away all those negative things you don't want in your life and replace them with love, you'll find yourself living a highly functioning life.

Receiving the orange that day, the very morning after my encounter with Wayne in the café with Anne, was to me a clear message. Not only did I know Wayne was with me, guiding and helping me, but I knew he was encouraging me to let go of the anger in my heart, and to forgive. To focus on the positive potential of love and hope and healing, and to leave sadness, hurt, anger, and regret behind. It was such a blessing, and I felt such gratitude this great teacher had shared some of his wisdom through a simple orange.

CHAPTER 26

Wendy Kelly
Dawn Hare

Being able to let go of a toxic relationship and acknowledge I deserved to be treated better was freeing. In leaving the relationship I learned to love myself more fully, and to trust my gut when it comes to love. I truly feel the experience opened me to a love the likes of which I had never allowed myself to receive. I did find love again—with a beautiful woman named Michelle—and our relationship is by far the healthiest and most balanced relationship of my life. Ours is truly a marriage of equals.

As I continue to evolve as a human, and as a medium, I'm constantly amazed at the new things the spirit world tosses my way. Recently, I was up early on a Saturday morning, doing one of my favourite things in the whole world: cooking a big breakfast of bacon and eggs. There I was, just flipping the bacon on the stove, feeling happy and grateful to be exactly where I was at that moment, when all of a sudden I heard a voice in my head: "Wendy."

"That's odd," I said out loud to Michelle. "Somebody just jumped into my head, and said their name was Wendy."

Before Michelle could even respond the voice said, "I know her."

"She says she knows you. Did you know anyone who passed named Wendy?"

"No, I don't think so." Michelle looked puzzled. "Wait a minute—I did know someone in junior high named Wendy. I think her last name was MacDonald. I'll check Facebook."

The smell of sizzling bacon filled the kitchen while Michelle pulled open her laptop. "Oh my gosh. Wendy died last year; exactly a year ago yesterday!"

Strangely, I had just posted a note on Facebook that same morning about acknowledging the deaths of loved ones on the anniversary of their death.

"Well, Wendy must be trying to let you know she's okay."

"That's nice," said Michelle, "but I didn't really know her all that well."

I continued to think about Wendy while I finished making breakfast, wondering why she had reached out to me, and thinking there had to be more to the story. I let it go and trusted more would be revealed—and I was right!

Later that day, we were driving home from an outing and Michelle asked why I thought Wendy might have reached out. "Do you think she's trying to let someone know she's okay? Do you think she's trying to pass on a message through you?"

"Seems like that may be the case." As soon as these words were out of my mouth I heard some other names in my head. I heard "Kelly" and "Don", and then I got an image of a woman dressed all in white, who was playing with her hair. She was pulling on it, as if she wanted to tell me something specific about her locks. When we got home we logged back onto Facebook and typed in combinations of the names I had heard. We found a Wendy Kelly MacDonald living in Kansas.

"That's where Wendy moved to!" said Michelle. "She was there for the last eight years." Michelle had been talking to a few friends who had stayed in touch with Wendy, so now she had a bit more information. "Maybe that's her husband, or her boyfriend, and they had a joint Facebook account with both their names?"

Thinking that may be the case I messaged this person on Facebook, trying to explain that I was a medium and had received a message from their deceased loved one. We didn't hear anything back during the night, and that line of inquiry felt like a dead end. I was very conscious Wendy wanted to get a message through, but we were barking up the wrong tree.

The next day, I sat at my computer and typed Wendy, MacDonald, Kelly, Don, and Kansas into a search engine. An obituary for a Wendy Kelly Dawn Hare popped up. I suddenly remembered the information I'd received in the car: the names Kelly and Don, which I mistakenly thought were men's names. I also recalled the image of the woman with shoulder-length, dirty blonde hair, (or "hare"), and felt she was trying to tell me something by tugging on it with her fingers. The Wendy MacDonald with whom Michelle had gone to school became Wendy Kelly Dawn Hare. She had died a year ago in Kansas.

In the obituary there was mention of a husband and a mother, so I went to both their Facebook pages. I didn't feel anything from the husband's, but when I got to the mother's page there was quite a sad message which had been written on the anniversary of her daughter's death, just two days ago. The mother's name was Cathy MacDonald, and she wrote about missing her daughter terribly and wishing she had a chance to say goodbye. She also wrote about how she was really struggling, and hoped to receive some sort of sign or message her daughter was okay.

    I became confident Wendy was indeed reaching out to me, via her connection with Michelle, in order to get a message to her mom. I privately messaged Cathy through Facebook, prefacing everything with, "I know this is going to sound crazy...." I told her I would love to talk over the phone because I was pretty sure her daughter Wendy was reaching out and wanted to get a message to her. I ended with, "I'm not looking for anything from you, and this won't cost you a cent. If you want to contact me here is my phone number."

    People who have died and who are now in the spirit world don't usually seek me out outside the context of a reading. This had never happened before—likely because I asked my guides to control who speaks to me, so as to not be bombarded by different and possibly demanding energies in the course of a regular day—but I felt Wendy's urgency, and I knew I had to at least *try*.

    After twenty-four hours Cathy did call. She assured me she had been incredibly suspicious, but had checked me out and felt I seemed "legit". I told her the whole story; about how her daughter Wendy came to be communicating with me. Her mother even had a little laugh at one point. "She was always really headstrong. It doesn't surprise me she found you!"

    "Your daughter wants to let you know she's okay. I believe she found me because she knows how much you're struggling with her death. She wants you to know she's doing well, and that she loves you so much. She's still with you. All you have to do is think of her, and she'll be right there."

    Cathy cried and thanked me. "You don't know how much this means to me," she said. "I've been asking for something like this, for a sign, and I feel like I've got it."

    I felt the great grief Wendy's mother had been holding

onto. I hoped hearing from her daughter would help ease the pain, going forward. In my opinion, there is no greater agony than losing a child, and I was happy I could help Cathy in this way.

This very unique situation was also rather meaningful personally. It was similar to my experience at Costco, with Dan and his mother Mildred, as in I felt as though I had been placed in just the right spot to help someone who really needed the service I could provide. I love that the Great Spirit knows I am open to being used for the greater good; that I can play a role in restoring a connection and helping to heal a grieving heart.

CHAPTER 27

Only a Thought Away

In the summer of 2017 I was at Michelle's home looking for things around the house I could fix or repair. I had discovered the screens in her bedroom and kitchen windows had many rips and tears. She explained her cat, Tiger, was the culprit, and it was behaviour typical of a kitten. I asked if she would mind if I replaced the screens.

"I would love for you to replace or fix them," she replied, "so I can open the windows again without fear of the cat escaping, not to mention letting in a cool breeze these summer evenings."

Prior to my next visit with Michelle I stopped at Home Depot and picked up a rubber insert and roll of screen mesh. Upon my arrival I slid out both window screens, removed the old ones, and proceeded to measure and cut the new material. I then laid the screen on the frame, and used the rubber insert to push it into the groove.

Michelle was in awe of how easy I made it look. "If I knew it was that easy I would have done it long ago." She then asked, "How do you know how to do this? Who taught you? Or is this a "guy thing", and you just know how?"

I laughed. "Funny you should ask. I remember, when I was about eleven years old, I was at a friend's house in Elmsdale—where I grew up. It was a bright, sunny day, and we had just come back from swimming in the Shubenacadie River. We were acting like kids, running around his house, when I had heard him run out onto their back deck. I ran after him, and couldn't see that the screen door was closed, due to it being dark inside and light outside.

I went crashing through and ripped the entire screen door out. Bruce, my friend's father, saw and picked me up and asked if I was okay. I was, but a little shaken as it had caught me by surprise. He then asked us to stop running around, and instructed that I would replace the screen on the door as soon as I could.

I went home and spoke to my father about what happened, but was a little nervous. My dad got angry sometimes, especially when I had done something reckless as a young boy. I was happily surprised he didn't get mad, but rather jumped into the family car and drove over to get mesh and a rubber insert from the local hardware store.

He dropped me off at my friend's house and waited for me in the car. I was met by Bruce, who requested I change the screen in the door myself. I pleaded with him, explaining I didn't know how. I had to run out to the car and get my father to show me how to do it. I was nervous about asking my father, and felt embarrassed for not being more aware of my surroundings at someone else's home.

My father came inside and proceeded to patiently show me, step by step, as I watched him remove and replace the screen in the door. I still felt a sense of relief, and gratitude, my dad wasn't angry. He just smiled, and asked Bruce if he was happy with the new screen. Bruce thanked us and said he was, but once again mentioned not running around the house in a kind, parenting manner. Dad and I jumped back in the car and went home.

After I told Michelle this story a few tears rolled down my cheek. At that moment I could feel my dad in my thoughts and in my heart. I knew he knew I was thinking and speaking about him. I could sense his spirit and awareness with mine.

Out loud I said, "Dad, I know you are with me, and it's been a long time since I have felt you this close. You have been gone almost thirty years, and I am still grateful we connect here and there. Thank you!"

We all have people we care about and miss dearly in the spirit world. We all have memories that just pop into our mind out of the blue. Often, people believe their thoughts are just that: thoughts. Imagine, the moment you think of someone in the spirit world, they know you are thinking of them—especially during those moments where you reflect and remember a specific time together.

So, from this day forward, please do yourself and the people in the light you care about a favour: acknowledge out loud, or in your mind, that you know they are with you. Open your mind, heart, and spirit, and feel them within and surrounding you. Feel the love you share for each other in that moment. Thank them!

Many people feel alone, but if you only knew who walks with you along your journey, you would never feel alone again. All your people, and all your animals, in the spirit world are only a thought away.

CHAPTER 28

A Visit from an Old Friend

Spending time with Michelle, and falling in love with my best friend, was the greatest feeling, the greatest gift, in the world. I am grateful to the Great Spirit for helping us find each other again. Fact is, Michelle and I had met seven years ago at a group reading she held at her home in East Chezzetcook, Nova Scotia. I remember thinking she was special at the time, and somebody would be very lucky to have her in their life.

After the relationship with me previous partner ended, I stood outside staring up towards the stars on New Year's Eve. It was December 31, 2016, and as the clock struck midnight I prayed and pleaded with my guides, with the angels, and with the Great Spirit to send the perfect person for me. I was tired of being hurt, and wanted somebody I could share my life journey with—and vice versa. Soon after, Michelle and I happened to run into each other at the grocery store, and after a year of being together got engaged. We purchased a property on the ocean, and plan on building a house, and a life, together.

Until then, I often stay over at her house. One such night I was in a deep slumber, cuddled right up to Michelle, when I began to dream. Ironically, I was at the grocery store once again. I was standing in the produce section, but could see down near the breads and baked goods. A man was walking toward me, becoming clearer as he got closer. I could see he was wearing a checkered shirt, and his hair was slicked over to the side. All at once, his face became clear.

"Oh my God," I said, "John; John McGrath! How are you? I haven't seen you in such a long time. It's got to be about seventeen years." John and I used to work together in the office of the furniture-manufacturing plant in Calgary. He just smiled and took his time as he walked right past me. John looked great, and younger than I remembered. He walked past a table where three women were sitting. As he did, everything seemed to turn into a restaurant and I became a waiter. I kept trying to get John to speak to me, but he continued walking past with his happy smile.

I woke up and said to Michelle, "Wow, I just dreamt of an old friend I used to work with in Calgary, about seventeen years ago. He was a great guy, and a Newfie (Newfoundlander) to boot. A long time ago I helped him set up a website for his band, The Dorymates. He played the accordion."

I grabbed my phone and began to google John McGrath, Calgary, and obituary, as he wasn't on my Facebook. In fact, I hadn't had contact with him since the day he retired. I soon discovered John James McGrath passed away two weeks ago—January 4, 2018, at the age of seventy-eight.

I was blown away by the fact he would come to visit and let me know he had made his transition into the light. We all lose contact with people, but never in a million years would I have thought I would find out somebody had moved into the spirit world this way. I am again thankful, and grateful, and know we were in each other's life for a reason. When my day comes I have a feeling he will be in the vast group of those waiting for me; to greet me and welcome me home.

I say this to many people: "None of us are getting out of this world alive." We all have a time to be here; to learn, to grow, and to evolve as a spirit. We are all simply spirits having a human experience—not the other way around.

Many can pass through our lives and not seem significant. However, we learn from every person who comes into our lives. We are all connected by the same goal: to help each other grow and accomplish what we need to while we are here. Some people do this in small ways, others in much greater ways. Some people can be our greatest teachers through great hardship, and others through great love.

CHAPTER 29

Signs from Spirit

People who have passed find all kinds of ways to communicate with those of us still living. It could be through a butterfly. It could be a dime. It could be a dragonfly. It may even be a feather or a rainbow or a dream. Sometimes it's a song on the radio or repeating numbers. For example, you might continually see 11:11 on a clock, or 222 on a licence plate. Either way, your loved ones will find a way of communicating via one or more of these signs. If you have many family members or close friends in the spirit world they will usually send different signs. I know it's my dad who sends dimes because of the image of the ship and his naval background. Also, the dimes I find are usually from 1987—the year he died.

Sometimes, people schedule an appointment to figure out who is behind the signs they are receiving. They come hoping I will validate the sign or symbol as that from a specific spirit.

I always tell them when I receive that image in my readings, but I'd like to say here you probably already know. Trust your intuition, your gut, and your heart. Your spirit already knows. In the sessions, I also sometimes ask clients to write down who they think is sending them a particular sign. I also write down who I know it is, based on my communication with the spirit world. Ninety-nine per cent of the time we've written the same name. They already knew, yet just wanted it confirmed.

Many people ask, "Why do I find so many dimes?" Dimes are light and easy for a spirit to move, so they are a common sign a spirit is with you. A few weeks after she met with me, one of my clients posted an amazing story on Facebook. During our session her father communicated to me that he sends his daughter dimes. She acknowledged she did find dimes from time to time, but nothing could have prepared her for what happened next. While readying her living room to put up the Christmas tree she moved an entertainment unit. Behind the unit was a cross, which had belonged to her father. What do you think was perched atop the cross? A dime! The cross had been behind the entertainment unit since the previous Christmas, so how could that possibly have happened without the assistance of a spirit?

Similarly, religious medallions are also light and easy to move. Another client posted a story to Facebook four months after we had met. During our session, four of her recently deceased relatives connected with me and told me they would be sending my client a religious medallion of some kind. Four months later, when she went to visit her brother's grave, there was a medallion of Archangel Michael sitting on his tombstone, waiting for her to find it.

The comfort these two women experienced when they received these signs is beyond measure. I love being able to help people understand spirits communicate with us all the time, letting us know they are eternally with us.

I also know, without a shadow of a doubt, that spirits listen when you desire a specific form of confirmation. Earlier, I wrote about how I asked for a sign from my dad, and knew I could count on him to send dimes and blue jay feathers. I also started to notice he would make sure that wherever I was, in the car, the dentist office, or the mall, I was sure to hear either "American Pie" or "The House of the Rising Sun"—two songs he had played on his guitar, and which he sang well.

Yet I was really curious about how far we could take this, so I decided to ask my father for something very specific and very unique. This is when I was still living in Calgary. I knew if he came through with the request it would be an incredible validation that he still heard me. I asked for a bird sighting, but not just any bird. I asked for a pure-white dove. Doves, after all, were not a common sight in Calgary! Soon after, I started to notice images of doves appearing on TV commercials, on billboards, and in photos. Once, I even saw one on a truck parked beside me in traffic: Two Doves moving company. I also recall having conversations with my father in which I said things like, "Dad, I know you're trying, but I don't want a picture of a dove. I want the actual thing. I want to see a real white dove."

Months passed. One day, I got a call to do a group reading at a house on the other side of Calgary. The city has a major highway which runs from one end to the other, called Deerfoot Trail, which is what I used to cross Calgary that day. As I drove I thought about the sign I'd asked my dad for, and how it hadn't yet appeared. I have to admit I was feeling a little disappointed. Just then, "The House of the Rising Sun" came on the radio and I remember thinking, *That's nice Dad, but I'm still waiting for my dove.* Just as the song was finished I was driving past the Bow River. I looked off to my left and saw a white bird. I was doing one hundred kilometres per hour, but the white flash of the bird piqued my curiosity. I kept stealing glances as I drove, and sure enough it appeared to be heading right for my car.

I was starting to get excited now because it was so white. I remember thinking, *Either that's a dove or it's the whitest pigeon I've ever seen.* I stole another glance, and as the bird got closer I realized with a start it was definitely a dove. Still, it kept coming. That dove ended up flying right beside my driver's side window! As if to seal the deal it looked me square in the eyes.

I was completely blown away, and immediately started to cry. My dad had come through with shining colours! The following song came on the radio, aptly called "It's Okay to Cry for Me". And so I did! I had set the bar high, but he delivered. I had got my sign.

I hope this story makes you aware you never have to go to a psychic medium in order to feel connected to loved ones who have passed on. They are right there, willing and able to communicate. I also want you to understand you don't need me, or someone like me, to validate these experiences for yourself. Intentionally connect with your loved ones, and tell them what you want. Visualize it in your mind. Be specific and be patient, and prepare to be astonished.

That dove came to me in the most powerful and unique way. I didn't even know if it was possible, but I still asked and believed I would receive. This extraordinary thing happened to me, and I believe I'm no more connected than anyone else—I am just more aware of my connection! So, please know you have that same connection to your people, your loved ones; to your ancestors in the spirit world. When they deliver their signs, remember to thank them. They like knowing you see the sign for what it actually is: direct communication. It's their way of saying, "Hey, I'm not that far away. I'm right here, visiting."

CHAPTER 30

The Language of Spirit

Over time I have discovered spirits are always communicating with us. They often do so in a way which most people don't recognize or remember. Yet theirs is a universal language every one of us has access to, and can learn. It's not a language you speak; it's a language of energy of which people in the physical world can become more aware. Everybody has these abilities, you just don't remember you do. The truth is we are all born psychic and connected to the spirit world, but with time our memories fade as we become more ingrained in the physical plane.

    This language is a way for spirits to communicate, guide, and validate messages of love. Doing so through a medium helps people find closure and healing, especially those who are struggling with their grief. The assistance of a medium is merely an extension to the healing process, but by no means should it be the first place you turn when facing a loss of a loved one.

If you're interested in trying to receive spirit messages I suggest you establish some rapport with the spirit world first. Address any spirits who may be around you. Tell them you're open, you're present, and you're available for communication with those in the light. Invite, and allow, the spirit world to send you information. Next, prepare yourself to receive these messages.

Before I do this work I ground myself through intention, prayer, and meditation. I also smudge myself to clear my energy and my space. These spiritual practices allow me to mentally and spiritually open up my awareness to receive, perceive, and share the spirit messages that do come through.

There are aspects of spirit communication and their language which can be referred to as the "clairs": clairvoyance, clairsentience, clairaudience, clairalience, claircognizance, and clairgustance. (Each of these I will discuss below.)

The first gift of the language is called clairvoyance, which means "clear seeing". These are visual impressions you see in your mind. If this feels difficult to understand, try this: while reading these words, imagine you are driving a car. It's a sunny day and the windows are down and there's a good song on the radio. Maybe you've got some change in the cup holder, and sunglasses on the passenger seat. You can see that, right? Now make it a little bit foggy—so the image isn't crystal clear—and remove yourself from this vision. Imagine you have no connection to the image in your mind. This is what it's like to be clairvoyant. It's as though you're simply observing the image infused into your mind. These messages are in the form of flowing images, coming at a speed in which you are able to understand. Often, I am looking off, with a blank, internal gaze; it's very much like allowing myself to daydream.

This is also how crystal balls work. The psychic using it doesn't actually see anything in it. They are simply giving their eyes a blank slate, so they could allow themselves to "see" the visual images flowing into their minds. In the past, the Mi'kmaq people would have stared into a bowl of water to achieve the same effect. During my readings I usually stare at the floor or the wall. There's nothing there, but staring without a focal point allows me to see the visual images which flow through my mind.

The visual images we receive can either be literal or symbolic. When I see an apple I know it could be a literal apple, or about somebody with the nickname apple. It could be symbolic, as in "An apple a day keeps the doctor away". So, in this case, the apple may be a message about health. Apples can also be symbols of teachers. How I see the image, but also *feel* it, helps me understand what it is the spirits are trying to say with the information they send. I'm aware, I observe, and I interpret and work with the given energy in order to allow that communication to happen.

I was live on Hay House radio with psychic medium John Holland as a guest. We had a caller on the line, for whom I saw the image of a little brown terrier dog. It was the same as I saw on TV as a kid, on a show called *Benji*. I asked the caller if she had a little brown terrier dog in the spirit world.

She said, "No!"

"This is strange," I replied. "I am seeing a TV show from when I was a kid, and it had a little brown terrier in it named Benji."

"My dad's name is Benji," she said after a moment, "and he is in the spirit world."

Through this clairvoyant image placed in my mind I was able to say her father's name.

Clairsentience is the next gift. It means "clear feeling" or "clear sensing". It also could be called intuition or a gut feeling, and is the one gift we've probably all felt. It's walking into someone's office and knowing they're having a bad day; it's walking down a dark street and sensing danger. This gift doesn't just come from the spirit world, rather, it's about energy. As we're all made of energy we can tune into someone else's living aura, someone's spiritual energy, in the light. You may even be able to feel somebody's personality and mannerisms.

I use clairsentience in my work to add depth and specificity to the images I see. Most readings I will actually feel the way in which someone passed: pressure in my chest usually means a heart attack; lung issues make me feel short of breath. There have even been times where fluid filled my lungs during a reading, and I actually had to cough the fluid up. Another time, someone who had had a stroke came through, and I began to drool out of the left side of my mouth. If someone was hard of hearing, or deaf in one ear, my ear would feel as though it's plugged with water. If somebody had vision issues, my eyes might go blurry for a second. If someone had a thyroid issue, I feel pressure in my throat.

Paying attention to our bodies, and what we feel, is clairsentience. If you'd like to experiment with this gift try becoming aware of how people you know are feeling, without them telling you. Try and feel out what is happening for them, and then ask to see if your feelings were correct. As you learn to trust this gift be brave and practice saying what you feel first, and then ask if you're correct. When connecting to a spirit in this way you may feel their personality, a masculine or feminine energy. You may also feel their love, peace, or concern for a loved one they see struggling in the physical world. Honour and trust all your feelings, however you may receive them.

If you're someone who felt a lot of anxiety as a child, and are still prone to anxiety as an adult, it's likely you have highly undeveloped clairsentient abilities. The trick is learning to ground yourself, and put such practices into place as surrounding yourself with love and light, and asking for emotional balance from your angels and guides to cement your intellect and your emotion. Smudging yourself, pray, and meditate. These practices will help with the sheer amount of information you are picking up, feeling, and processing. If you feel called to be a healer learning how to manage this energy is essential, and it will enable you to help others more effectively.

Another important aspect of the language of spirit is clairaudience, which means "clear hearing". When I first started doing this work this ability was one of the first to manifest. As you'll remember, from the stories I told earlier, there was a time I worried I was schizophrenic because I was hearing names in my head which I couldn't control. Over the last twenty years I've worked to develop this gift, and now it is the ability which most often helps to validate the presence of a loved one. When I can give my clients the actual name of the person communicating with them from the other side it makes a huge difference.

When spirits talk to us in a way we can hear it isn't typically through long-winded speeches. Rather, it's more like quick little bursts of audible voice or thought. It may be a name, a date, or a meaningful word. As you practice, you will learn to discern the sound of your own mental voice from that of spirit. I like to think of the voice of spirit as a quieter, smaller one behind my own that wants to guide us in some way, or draw our attention to something.

To help, count to ten slowly, then add in the alphabet. (1a, 2b, 3c, 4d, 5e, 6f, 7g, 8h, 9i, 10j.) Now, in your mind, speak *Jim, Mary, Joy, Margaret*. When spirits speak it is soft and subtle, and could easily be missed if you are not mentally focused and aware of your thoughts.

Once in a while I actually hear a voice out loud; like the

time in Halifax's Point Pleasant Park with the pirate, and where I recorded my spirit guide Victoria speaking to me. This has also happened in client sessions, when I clearly hear another voice in the room. When I listen back, the voice I heard has also been captured on the digital recorder.

As you practice clear hearing, be aware that if you hear anything negative or frightening it is not coming from the light. Spirits guide us from a place of love, and only love.

Although the next three gifts are less common, they are no less interesting and valuable.

Claircognizance means "clear knowing", usually without words or reason. Examples of this gift are quite simple, and sometimes dramatic. Like the person who just knew they shouldn't get on the airplane, which then crashes. As in someone who knew when they heard the phone ring their daughter was calling to say she was pregnant. In my experience this gift does not happen all the time, but when it does it's very enlightening.

Clairalience, or clairscent, means "clear smelling", and can be a very surprising when it happens to you. On the morning of the twenty-ninth anniversary of my dad's passing I woke up and smelled intense cigarette smoke. It was as though someone had just taken a big drag off a cigarette and blew it right in my face. It was physically not possible—no one smoked in our house—but it was overpowering and real. I knew my dad, who had been a smoker, was paying a visit! During client readings I will sometimes suddenly smell flowers or perfume or cigars. I've come to learn it is simply part of the conversation. Spirits find all kinds of different ways to communicate who they are in order to validate their presence to a loved one.

Clairgustance means "clear tasting", and occurs when you taste something without actually putting anything into your mouth. I once experienced this during a live radio show. I was connecting to the radio host's grandmother, and all I could taste was cake. When I told him he confirmed his grandmother had to have cake for every occasion. "She wouldn't come unless there was cake," he laughed.

All of these gifts are aspects of the language of spirit, and I consider myself a good spirit translator. I hope this chapter has convinced you that you too can become a translator for your own life and spirit connections. As you read the above, my guess is you felt more resonance with some over the others. Am I right? I feel equally balanced in clairvoyance, clairsentience, and clairaudience because of how often they occur in my work. Your gift may be more clairsentience, for example. Whichever is your most prominent gift work with it and develop it, and learn to trust it. I promise the others will follow.

Don't get discouraged if, and when, you receive information you don't understand. It happens to me all the time! Even after twenty years I'm still very much learning, and I feel like spirit is constantly expanding my vocabulary. I want to encourage you to trust the information of which you are unsure—the meaning may reveal itself later. I've learned to sometimes just tell my clients what I'm seeing or feeling or hearing because undoubtedly, even if it doesn't make any sense to me, they usually know exactly what I'm talking about.

Finally, it's important to remember to always set an intention for only good to flow from what you receive. If you're starting to work with other people as a healer be clear your wish is to help people. Before I do readings for anyone I tell my spirit guides I'm open, I'm ready, and I'm willing to receive the messages that will be communicated through me, however they come through. I completely let go of any expectation of how the information should come, and I work with whatever flows through my awareness.

I wish you joy and delight as you begin to learn the language of spirit!

CHAPTER 31

Intention

Psychics and mediums have access to all kinds of information. If you wish to develop your gift you need to be very clear with your guides about what you want to hear and see. This work should be about helping and guiding people, and giving them reassurance. It should never be about frightening them. I like to think of this as psychic etiquette; always working with integrity.

We've all heard stories about someone who has visited a psychic only to be told a loved one was going to be badly injured, or even die. It's one of the main reasons many people say they would never go and see a psychic. They don't want to be told something bad will happen to them, or someone they love. They don't want to hear something they will have no control over.

I have my own stories about this. A few years ago, when I was still in my first marriage, I woke up one morning with the name Vivian being spoken in my head. When I asked Marissa if she knew someone by that name she said the only Vivian she knew was a psychic in Dartmouth. At the time, I was considering going to someone for a bit of guidance about my marriage. Yet I tend to be a big skeptic of other mediums because I've met so few who are authentic. I thought because her name popped into my head it was a sign I should go see her.

I made an appointment, but used a different name because I didn't want her to know who I was. The first thing Vivian had me do was to drink a cup of tea. She then read the tea leaves left in the bottom. I was intrigued because my great-grandmother had also been a tea-leaf reader. Vivian then used some tarot cards, but nothing she told me resonated with my situation. I had really gone with the intention of receiving guidance about my relationship, so I was disappointed not to get any.

I started to wonder if the real reason I was brought to meet Vivian was to do a reading for her. I told her who I was, and was able to bring her some messages from the spirit world. She seemed very touched, but as I was leaving another piece of information came through. I strongly felt and saw that Vivian would have a bad fall.

I didn't want to alarm her, but I did want her to know what I was seeing so she could protect herself. I assumed my guides were showing me this information so I could help keep Vivian safe. I sensed the fall would be in her own home, so I asked her to take me on a tour of her house. I was able to identify two areas—the basement stairs and the shower in the bathroom—as places where she needed to be extra careful. I could tell she hadn't really taken the warning to heart, and I left feeling a little brushed off. I told myself there was nothing else I could do but share the information, so I let it be. A couple of months has passed when I heard Vivian was in the hospital because she had fallen in the tub. She was in a coma. Two days later she died.

I wasn't surprised, due to the clarity of the information I had received, but I was deeply troubled and quite angry with my guides. Why would they wake me up to tell me this woman's name if I couldn't actually keep her from having the accident which killed her? After, I gave my guides clear instructions to never again allow me to see something I wouldn't be able to change. I never want to be right about someone dying. If you are developing these skills yourself I highly recommend you give your guides solid direction about what kind of information you would like to receive.

Nothing like that has ever happened again, yet sometimes I am given information about mishaps or injuries. For instance, I was once reading a woman and connecting to her parents who were both in the spirit world. She asked if they were around her son, who was a young adult and just starting university in another province. As I connected to his energy I suddenly felt an intense pain in my jaw. I asked her if he had had surgery, or any major dental work done on his teeth. She said he had braces when he was younger, but now had perfect teeth and no injuries related to his jaw. I told her if anything happened where her son hurt his jaw she should know her parents would be with their grandson.

A month or two later she sent an email to tell me her son had been attacked outside a bar, and now had a badly broken jaw requiring reconstructive surgery. The woman thanked me, and said knowing her parents were with him had made all the difference during this difficult time.

A similar thing happened during another reading at one of Halifax's psychic fairs. When the woman sat in front of me the first thing I knew was she was the mother of a young man who was currently in the military. She confirmed he had just gone to Kuwait, and I clearly got an image of a landmine. I also got the information he was going to be affected, but okay. I told her I knew this wasn't the best news to receive at a psychic fair, and I certainly didn't want to be right about it, but I had a strong feeling it would happen. When she wrote me a few months later to confirm her son had been injured in a road side bomb explosion she also said that knowing he wasn't going to die made all the difference in the world.

The purpose of this chapter is to let you know your spirit guides listen when you give them directions. I've never had another experience like that with Vivian again. I can feel coming illness or accidents with my clients, but it's always in situations where I'm able to give specific guidance on what needs to shift or change. I always let people know I'm not a doctor, but I am able to see things. I then direct them to find a specialist who can help with the issue I've picked up.

CHAPTER 32

Native Culture and Spirituality

We are all one, and come from the same source. All faiths and belief systems are a way to source energy. It's divine love which unites us all and unites all beliefs. In the Native culture, all ceremonies are done to honour the Great Spirit, as well as our ancestors, through language and prayers. They are our ways, and our words, for connecting to the creator.

I am grateful for my Mi'kmaq culture, and for its teachings about our connection to the natural and spiritual world. These teachings aren't something I grew up with, as I was raised in the Catholic Church and had only occasional visits with my Newfoundland grandmother as a child. It was only when I became an adult, and began to work as a psychic medium, that I began to learn more about my own culture. Different teachers have shared their knowledge and wisdom, and I'm deeply appreciative to all. However, I'm still learning and by no means am I an Elder. My work connecting to spirits has nothing to do with my culture, but I like to incorporate my culture into the work I do. So, this chapter is about some of the traditions I now use in my own life, as well as to help other people.

That said, the most fundamental of these practices is the expression of gratitude. In Indigenous culture there is always some sort of thanks given. The Mi'kmaq word for thank you is *wela'lin*. We thank *Kisu'lk* (creator); we thank Grandfather Sun, we thank Mother Earth, we thank all the species upon the Earth. When you're taking the life of a tree to make a canoe, you thank the tree; when you take the life of an animal to nourish yourself, you thank that animal. This thanks is traditionally given through tobacco because it is the most sacred medicine used for ceremonial offerings.

Smudging

Smudging has become an integral part of my life, and in my work with clients. I would like to share this practice with those who might like to try smudging. In our culture there are four sacred medicines one can use: tobacco, cedar, sage, and sweetgrass (also known as mother's hair). Place the medicine in a shell or a pottery dish—it should be something of the earth. Light it, blow it out, and then pull the smoke over the top of your head, asking the Great Spirit to help you to know the truth. Next, pull the smoke into your eyes and ask the Great Spirit to help you to see the truth. Then pull the smoke into your ears and ask the Great Spirit to help you hear the truth. After, pull the smoke into your mouth and your nose, without inhaling, and ask the Great Spirit to help you speak and breathe the truth. Lastly, pull the smoke into your heart and ask the Great Spirit to help you feel the truth. To finish, cleanse your whole body by moving the smoke over your arms and legs.

Smudging is something you can do on your own to great benefit. Other traditional Native ceremonies, such as the pipe ceremony, the sweat lodge, the vision quest, the naming ceremony, and the talking circle should be taught by a trained Elder. Please, if you take the time to learn something from an Elder, don't take the teaching and make it your own by changing the practice. Respect the teaching as it is; respect it as it was taught.

There are many men and women who are great teachers, especially in the Mi'kmaq culture. I have been very fortunate to be the recipient of some of their teachings. Ours is a culture of working together and caring for your fellow brothers and sisters, your aunts and uncles, your mothers, your fathers, your grandmothers, your grandfathers, and your cousins. We are all related.

Totem

Spirit animal totems are also important to Indigenous culture. We all have a spirit animal totem which help guide us on our path, and help provide answers to questions. Spirit animals such as the *Kitpu* (Eagle), *Muin* (Bear), *Tiam* (Moose), or perhaps the *Kokokwes* (Owl) has a certain strength with which you strongly resonate. They may show up in your life as a sign, or in a dream, to show you something important.

Drum

For centuries, Indigenous people have believed the drum and the heart share a similar purpose: to provide life through its beat. This connection promotes oneness between people and nature, and promotes love and respect for all living things. The Mi'kmaq people believe the drum is the heartbeat of Mother Earth. There are many ceremonial songs which include the drum; my favourite is "The Honour Song," which can be found on YouTube here: https://youtu.be/MNf1FLW7D0U

The Medicine Wheel

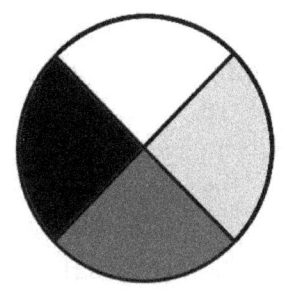

The medicine wheel represents all of creation, and the inner connectedness of all people and things. I have read, and have been taught, different teachings by different Elders, and have come the conclusion there is no right way, nor one Indigenous culture that has it "right". Although I have tried to incorporate as much Mi'kmaq teaching as I can, I believe it is best to look at the medicine wheel teachings in a personal light.

The wheel's shape represents creation, the circle of life with no beginning and no end. It shows we are all one people together; united, we are all one. All Mi'kmaq ceremonies start in the east quadrant, with the rising sun. From there, all ceremonies are completed in a clockwise direction to follow the sun, moving to the south, the west, and lastly to the north.

The four colours—yellow, red, black, and white—represent many things. They represent the four seasons, spring, summer, fall, winter; they represent the four medicines, tobacco, cedar, sage, and sweetgrass they represent the four stages of life, infancy, youth, adulthood, and elder; they represent the four aspects of human personality, spiritual, emotional, physical, and mental; they represent the four elements, fire, water, earth, and air; and finally, they represent the four colours of the people of the world, Asian (yellow), Indigenous (red), African (black), and Caucasian (white).

Along with the medicine wheel there are also a seven directional teachings. (Seven is a sacred number to the Mi'kmaq people.) The seven sacred teachings of love, respect, courage, humility, honesty, wisdom, and truth are very important traditional values which will help you live a good life.

Honour the four directions by facing them as listed above then look upwards and face the sky and spirit world, honouring the creator. Look toward the earth and honour our mother. Look within and honour yourself and your journey and your spirit.

East/Yellow: Spring, tobacco, infancy, spirituality, fire, Asians; love and respect.
South/Red: Summer, cedar, youth, emotions, water, Indigenous peoples; courage.
West/Black: Fall, sage, adulthood, physical, earth, Africans; honesty and humility.
North/White: Winter, sweetgrass, elders, air, Caucasians; wisdom and truth.

A Mi'kmaq Prayer.

Msit No'kmaq, all my relations. I honour you in the circle of life today. I am grateful to acknowledge you in this prayer.

Kisu'lk, creator, for the ultimate gift of life; *wela'lin*, thank you.

Nisgam, Grandfather Sun, for the ultimate gift of my spirit and my shadow; *wela'lin*, thank you.

Ogijinew, Mother Earth for the mineral nation which has built my body and maintained my bones and all foundations of my physical life and experience; *wela'lin*, thank you.

To the Plant Nation which sustains my organs, my body, and gives me healing herbs for sickness; *wela'lin*, thank you.

To the Animal Nation which feeds me and offers me companionship in this walk of life; *wela'lin*, thank you.

To Osgijinew, the people who share my path upon the sacred wheel of this earthly life; *wela'lin*, thank you my brothers and sisters.

To the Spirit Nation which guides me through the ups and downs, and shows me the light in everything through it all; *wela'lin*, thank you.

In all seven directions, thank you. You are all my relations, my relatives, and without whom I would not live. We are in the circle of life together, coexisting, codependent, co-creating our destiny. We are one nation evolving from the other, and yet dependent on the Great Spirit and the universe above and the Mother Earth below. I honour myself and my spirit in all four directions: East, South, West, North. All of us are one with the Great Spirit. *Wela'lin*, thank you for our lives and the love and light that we share. *Msit No'kmaq*, all my relations.

CHAPTER 33

Your Journey

From my heart to yours, I thank you for reading this book. I've felt called to write the story of my life (up to now!) for a long time, and am very grateful to you for being my witness. My intention for this book has always been to help you, the reader, learn from my journey. I hope I have inspired you to follow your own path, whatever it may be.

I want to close this book by saying I believe we all have a purpose on this earth. I would like to encourage you to really listen to the guidance being offered, and to honour it. Follow your heart, follow your dreams. Don't fight against the things your heart truly tells you to do. If you feel like you need to make a change, do it and don't wait. If you're not happy where you are, change the circumstances of your life. Don't live in fear!

I've learned, through my conversations with those in the spirit world, that our lives go by incredibly fast. A lifetime might feel long, but it's really not. Live your life to the fullest and engage in every moment as a gift of love from our creator. Find the ways to truly *live* your life. Don't just go through the motions. Don't live according to someone else's expectations. Don't put off hard conversations. Don't settle for less than you deserve.

Love yourself, and your journey, unconditionally. For many it appears as though we must make a choice at a crossroad. Yet in my life there has always been only one clear road: the one I was always meant to follow. If you are aware you will see yours the same way. Yet if you are not sure where or what your road is? Ask our creator: How may I be of service to others? How may I help change the world with my light and wisdom?

Ask every day until your answer comes. Walk your road, and do it with all your heart, mind, body, and spirit.

I'm so grateful to be able to share my experiences and wisdom with you. I hope you'll follow my continued journey, and I look forward to meeting you one day. Love and light to you my friend.

Thank you, I'll see you again. All my relations.

Wela'lin, ap nmu'ltes. Msit No'kmaq.

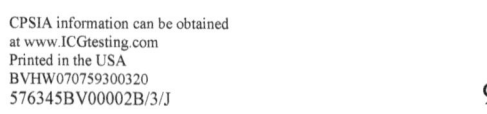